Debunking the Myth of America's Poodle

Why Great Britain Wants War

T0169233

Debunking the Myth of America's Poodle

Why Great Britain Wants War

Nu'man Abd al-Wahid

Winchester, UK
Washington, USA

JOHN HUNT PUBLISHING

First published by Zero Books, 2020
Zero Books is an imprint of John Hunt Publishing Ltd., No. 3 East St., Alresford,
Hampshire SO24 9EE, UK
office@jhpbooks.com
www.johnhuntpublishing.com
www.zero-books.net

For distributor details and how to order please visit the 'Ordering' section on our website.

Text copyright: Nu'man Abd al-Wahid 2018

ISBN: 978 1 78535 920 0
978 1 78535 921 7 (ebook)
Library of Congress Control Number: 2018965943

A CIP catalogue record for this book is available from the British Library.

Design: Stuart Davies

UK: Printed and bound by CPI Group (UK) Ltd, Croydon, CR0 4YY
US: Printed and bound by Thomson-Shore, 7300 West Joy Road, Dexter, MI 48130

We operate a distinctive and ethical publishing philosophy in
all areas of our business, from our global network of authors to
production and worldwide distribution.

Contents

Preface

An alternative title for this book would be *Everything that a British anti-war Movement has ever Told you is Wrong* but modesty and brevity dictate otherwise. The reason for writing the essays contained in this short book are two-fold. Firstly, to provide an alternative historically driven narrative on why the British establishment is in a state of constant eagerness to militarily intervene in foreign countries. This narrative is rooted in the British Empire's rise and fall and as the title suggests certainly not in the supposed loyalty to the so-called "special relationship" with the United States. Secondly, the book, I hope, provides a brief introduction to why and how the British establishment founded an empire.

Therefore, on one level the book should furnish the reader with a constructive rebuttal to a British anti-war movement's 60-year insistence that Great Britain is a "poodle" to the United States. On another layer of reading I have, once again, hopefully provided the reader with a solid foundational springboard to understand how the imperial legacy of the British Empire lives on in today's wars. Indeed, one of the unspoken but greatest achievements of the British establishment must be how the subject of British imperialism is absent from academic study at undergraduate level or even post-graduate level. It is a fact that one would be hard pressed to find a module on a Politics, History or International Relations course at undergraduate degree level that focuses on the 400-year-old British Empire let alone a dedicated degree.

I would like to thank the following individuals for their assistance in reading parts of this book. Firstly, Dr. Clive Harris who I have, on many occasions, interrupted as he was engaged in his own research at the Library of Birmingham. Max Ajl and Mudhusree Mukerjee for their feedback on the essay(s) I sent

1

to them. My appreciation also goes to the staff at John Hunt Publishing for agreeing to publish this book.

Finally, my warmest gratitude to the staff at the Library of Birmingham and my local library in Cradley Heath for their assistance. The latter assisted me immensely with obtaining many articles and books from the British Library and elsewhere.

Chapter 1

Introduction: Great Britain Wants War

The suicide terrorist massacre took the lives of 22 people, mostly children, at a pop music concert in Manchester in May 2017. The bomber had grown up in the city with his parents who had, we are strongly led to believe, "fled" Libya during the era of Colonel Muammar Gaddafi's rule. His parents had clearly settled in Manchester because there had already been a small but established community of Libyans residing there since the mid-1990s. And some of these Libyans were associated or members of a jihadi organisation, Libyan Islamic Fighting Group (LIFG).

Initially, the LIFG was made up of veterans from the so-called Afghan "jihad" whereby Islamist mercenaries were recruited from around the world to fight the Soviet Union's military intervention in Afghanistan in the 1980s. Out of this geo-political wash emerged a group of fighters known as the Arab-Afghans, that is fighters of Arab origin who travelled to fight Soviet troops in Afghanistan. Once the war was over, most of these fighters returned to their home countries but others sought refuge elsewhere in the knowledge that their home countries would be far from hospitable to their resettlement. Some Libyan and other veterans of this war found refuge in the United Kingdom.

The real reason behind British hospitality towards Libyan jihadis is that Libya had been a thorn in the British establishment's side ever since Colonel Gaddafi overthrew the British puppet King Idris in 1969. Gaddafi did not endear himself to Britain for nationalising the oil industry and his widely reported support for the Irish resistance in the northern part of Ireland. So it was no surprise that in 1996, Britain's foreign intelligence service, MI6, turned to a leader from the LIFG, a certain Abu Abdullah Sadiq, for assistance in an assassination attempt on Gaddafi.[1]

3

Sadiq was an alias of Abdel-Hakim Belhadj.

A leaked cable from the mid-1990s[2] revealed that the assassination attempt on Colonel Gaddafi was to be complemented by orchestrated uprisings in Libyan cities led by Libyan colonels with "limited contact" to Islamist-jihadi veterans of the war against the Soviet Union in Afghanistan. This plot failed but the plan certainly chimes with what materialised in the lead up to the NATO intervention of 2011.

The so-called "Arab Spring" of early 2011, that is the overthrow of the pro-Western Tunisian and Egyptian regimes, provided the British establishment with the perfect pretext to finally overthrow Colonel Gaddafi. Certain militias had quickly taken up arms against the government during the early stages of the Libyan "uprising." Gaddafi, in turn, made televised threats against these militias. For their part, Western media erroneously and falsely reported that Libyan army soldiers were committing rape crimes and employing foreign "African" mercenaries to recapture territory lost to the Islamist militias. Yet the only known foreigners in the early period of the uprising were captured British MI6 agents in Libya's second city, Benghazi.[3]

Overlooked in the early period of the rebellion was not only the racist lynching of black Libyans and Sub-Sahara African migrant workers by some of the Islamist militias but also the fanatical calls in the British media, especially its right-wing media, for the United States to lead a military intervention in Libya.

Libya

The following is an account of the calls to intervene in Libya with a deliberate focus on the main bugles of Britain's right-wing media, the *Daily Telegraph* and *The Times* because by virtue of circulation figures, at least, they are the most consequential. A mere 11 days after the uprising, 26 February 2011, the British media reported that there was a British and French plan to impose sanctions on Libya at the United Nations.[4]

In the week commencing 28 February 2011, the British media stepped up the tempo to promote military intervention. In *The Times*, Defence Editor Deborah Haynes reported that "Britain was ready to use force." [5] The report went on to say that: "Going further than any world leader, [UK Prime Minister] David Cameron said yesterday that he had ordered General Sir David Richards, the Chief of the Defence Staff, to work on how to impose a no-fly zone in Libyan airspace. Fighter jets would shoot down any encroaching Libyan aircraft..."

In the *Telegraph*, the British urge to drop bombs on Libya was dressed up as a Western initiative to do so: a report claimed that the, "West is ready to Use Force against Gadhaffi" because for Cameron, "...Gaddafi's departure was Britain's 'highest priority,'" adding: "If helping the opposition would somehow bring that about, it is certainly something we should be considering."[6]

As such certain individuals close to the British military informed the readership that it was ready for a "Libyan mission."[7]

British plans for intervention hit a stumbling block according to Christopher Hope of the *Daily Telegraph*, when other world leaders shunned the idea.[8] A spotlight was then placed on what the right-wing media perceived to be then President Obama's foot dragging. British militarism was not then keen on Obama sensing his paternal Kenyan roots as an impediment to mutual understanding because Imperial Britain had once occupied Kenya with the usual attendant repressions and torture. As such Obama was clearly singled-out as an obstacle to the British urge for military intervention or rather a no-fly zone.

"Waiting for Washington" declared *The Times* in late February 2011 as it praised the "success" of George W. Bush and Tony Blair in the "War on Terror" and compared their decisiveness and clarity with Obama's "hesitancy."[9] In another editorial entitled the "Essence of Indecision" the paper urged Obama to show "leadership" and referred to ex-Defence Secretary Robert Gates's rebuke of Cameron's call for military intervention as "inglorious." Naturally, because the Obama administration wasn't then keen on war it was accused of "sowing discord" among the Western alliance while the right-wing media also insubstantially accused Gaddafi of using foreign mercenaries and child soldiers.[10]

On 10 March 2011, *The Times* confirmed that it is Britain that is taking the lead in wanting intervention and delightedly declared that there is a "glimmer of hope" in the Obama administration in that it may be coming round to seeing the Libyan situation their way: "[with]British and French officials seeking quicker action from the US, the White House distanced itself for the first time from a policy tied to UN approval, creating a chance for rapid movement after indecision by the White House."[11]

On the following day, 11 March, a report in the *Daily Telegraph* openly queried the nature of Obama's strategy, "Is it cowardice? Is it indecisiveness? Or is it clever diplomacy?", before concluding that because of "America's size and military power, the American president does not have the option to remain neutral indefinitely..."[12] As we all know, Great Britain has always known what's best when it comes to what direction American foreign policy should take.

A comment piece, in the *Sunday Telegraph* on 13 March, contrasted Cameron's urge to intervene in Libya with Obama's "paralysis." The author goes on to "hope" that Obama "follows Cameron's lead, as Clinton followed Blair's lead in Kosovo." However, the writer does possess the honesty to argue that intervention is in Britain's interests: "The argument for intervention in Libya is not purely or even primarily humanitarian, however. Even if one sets aside its importance as an oil-producing nation, Libya remains central to Britain's strategic and commercial interests in the region."[13]

It is only natural that the *Daily Telegraph* editorialised over the next couple of days that Obama's "silence" is "hurting the West" (the "West" here is a generic metaphor meaning British interests). One of the ways the silence is hurting the "West" is that: "...staying out of other people's quarrels in the most volatile and oil-rich region on the planet is not a realistic foreign policy."[14]

Exactly! Realism can here clearly be defined as UK interests sitting on top of the oil wells of Libya.

On 16 March, *The Times* once again accused Obama of dithering or as it says, Obama "hovers and havers" while the British are resolute in purpose and as such are attempting "to get support for more robust action."[15]

Almost synchronically, both *The Times* and the *Daily Telegraph* reported that Cameron was finding it "frustrating" working with Obama.[16] One must surely ask, did the journalists who regurgitated Cameron's feelings in their respective newspaper reports sit at the same governmental briefing meeting?

The Times on 17 March, in an editorial, claimed that Obama was nowhere to be seen, and also seemed to be threatening that there would be "consequences" for his treatment of European opinion. They further argued, not for the first time, that Obama had been a "brutal disappointment."[17]

That is, he was a disappointment to the British urge for war on Libya.

On the same day *The Times* included a report which confirmed that it was Britain and France which had taken the lead in tabling the UN resolution to implement a no-fly zone.

Enough pressure seems to have been exerted on Obama by not only the British but also members within his own administration to intervene. The United Nations adopted a no-fly zone over Libya which was clearly and practically interpreted (or misinterpreted) by NATO as the spearhead of the "rebels" as they consolidated their positions in Benghazi and advanced into Tripoli before pulverising Gaddafi's hometown Sirte with

Apache helicopters.

It was known all along that the "rebels" included a good proportion of Islamists and specifically members of the al-Qaeda affiliated LIFG. In effect, a de facto alliance between NATO air power and Islamist militias emerged in 2011.

The Manchester suicide bomber's father, Ramadan Abedi, travelled to Libya to join in the British-led war during this period on the back of Britain's cries for intervention. His sons followed him.

We rightly remember the victims of the suicide bomber in Manchester but nothing of the millions of victims of the British-led intervention in Libya. Tens of thousands of Libyans were reported killed because of the intervention and millions of refugees were created, many now wanting to escape the lawlessness of Libya via the Mediterranean Sea.

Libya is now literally a violent no man's land. Whereas once it was one of the richest countries in Africa with excellent facilities and quality of life, it is now overrun by competing Islamist militias. Even an official British Parliamentary report on the intervention in Libya, published in 2016, conceded in conclusion that stories of Gaddafi's supposed atrocities, which were used to justify the no-fly zone, could not be confirmed or, as it says, it "could not verify the actual threat to civilians posed by the Ghadhaffi regime; it selectively took elements of Muammar Ghadhaffi's rhetoric at face value..." Furthermore, the report claimed that the government "failed to identify the militant Islamist extremist element in the rebellion."

At the end of the day, the report grudgingly admitted the intervention was based on "erroneous assumptions." In other words, Libya was destroyed in collusion with Islamist jihadis on the basis of a pack of lies.[18]

To rub salt into the wounds, Boris Johnson, as UK Foreign Secretary, was cracking jokes in late 2017 at Libya's expense claiming that no sooner than dead bodies could be removed from Libya's coastline the city of Sirte (Muammar Gaddafi's home town) could be turned into a new Dubai; that is, as we shall see later in the book, an outlet for British neo-colonialism.[19]

Syria

The Libyan intervention did not deter the British establishment from calling for more military intervention elsewhere, namely in Syria. Indeed, getting rid of Gaddafi only seemed to have whetted the appetite of Cameron.

As the Islamist militias were establishing themselves in Libya and reducing what was once a highly functional state to an anarchic pulp, Cameron visited the United States. Before he set off he was interviewed by arch-British imperialist apologist, historian Professor Niall Ferguson for *Newsweek* magazine in March 2012. Lo and behold, he once again announced his "frustration" at Washington's lack of interest in intervening in Syria.[20]

In the aftermath of Obama's re-election in November 2012, Cameron twice raised the verbal stakes in advocating intervention in Syria. Firstly, on the very day of Obama's historic re-election and on the back of peddling weapons to the Persian Gulf despots, he said he would advocate to his "friend" Obama that the situation in Syria be dealt with.[21]

In the following month Cameron rehashed the "inaction is not an option" formula as an argument to intervene in the Syrian war.[22] This formula dates back to the build-up for the war on Iraq in 2003 and was popularised by then Vice-President Dick Cheney who in turn adopted it from the military historian Victor Davis Hanson.[23]

Days later Cameron was claiming that his government was leading the calls to review the arms embargo on Syria with a view to supplying more weapons to the so-called "rebels."[24] It was also acknowledged that the British alongside the French had complained to the Obama administration about the latter preventing Qatar from sending more sophisticated weaponry to these rebels.[25] Clearly Qatar was the local surrogate for European strategies.

Iraq

Obviously Cameron's palpable hunger for war in Libya and Syria was simply in line with his most famous predecessor, Tony Blair. But there was a major difference in the way Cameron and Blair's approach to war was reported mainly because the British establishment would not or could not accept that Blair was behaving in accordance with what he thought were British interests and not because, as it was widely reported back then, due to his subservience to then American president, George W. Bush.

On the basis, of this wrongly perceived subservience, Tony Blair was dubbed a "poodle." As we shall see, it is not the first time in the post-World War Two era that the demeaning sobriquet has been pinned on a British Prime Minister when he or she is perceived to be in lock-step with American imperialism.

Indeed, one could argue that back in 2002-3 when Bush's America was making the case for war on Iraq on the back of misleading information about "weapons of mass destruction" (WMD) in the possession of Saddam Hussein's government falling into the hands of Islamist terrorists, the British establishment was no less committed to providing fabrications of its own to support the case for war. The UK government had claimed that Iraq could deploy WMD within "45 minutes"[26] and that Iraq had made "Uranium purchases from Niger."[27]

However, it needs to be emphasised that the erroneous notion that Tony Blair was simply being subservient, i.e. "a poodle," was propagated mostly by those who were against the war on Iraq, namely the leading organisers behind the UK anti-war movement, the "Stop the War Coalition" (StWC).

The prominent leaders of this movement, mostly left-wingers, the late Tony Benn, Andrew Murray, John Rees and Lindsey German had all made comments that British foreign policy was beholden to Bush's America. The Labour politician Tony Benn claimed that the UK waged war and invaded Iraq at the "behest" of the US government.[28] Andrew Murray claimed that Britain was "dragged" into the Iraq invasion,[29] while Lindsey German ridiculously claimed that British foreign policy was "dictated" by George W. Bush.[30] There was no evidence for any of these statements. The notion that Britain invaded Iraq purely with its own historical and economic interests in mind was clearly alien to these campaigners.

One of the anti-war movement's more mainstream advocates was the then *Guardian* newspaper's associate editor Seamus Milne who is now Labour leader Jeremy Corbyn's Strategy and Communications Director. He continually pushed the "poodle" line during the build-up for aggression on Iraq. The articles he wrote in this period are contained in his very commendable book *The Revenge of History*. As a disclaimer and because I don't want to be regarded as a hypocrite, I enjoyed reading this highly informative book but his insistence that Blair was subservient to Bush in the run-up to war on Iraq mustn't go unanswered.

A year before the 9/11 attacks on American soil and the subsequent announcement of a "War on Terror," Milne wrote an excellent and aptly titled article "Throwing our weight about."[31] Herein, he took to task Tony Blair's infatuation with military interventionism (or "humanitarian war") specifically in Kosovo, Iraq (1998) and Sierra Leone as well as noting British interference in Zimbabwean domestic issues. Milne further endorses Nelson Mandela's opinion of Blair, that is, he is "introducing chaos into international affairs," and informs his readers that Blair's "government has emerged as the most interventionist British administration since decolonisation." Most of all, he hits the nail on the head when he claims Blair's Chicago address in 1999 was a "clarion call...for a new wave of worldwide intervention."[32]

But no sooner had George W. Bush launched the so-called "War on Terror" on the back of the 9/11 terrorist attacks, than Milne seemed compelled for some strange reason to change his tune with regard to Blair's hunger for war. Rather than simply stating that Blair had found a political soul-mate with more military tools at his disposal, Milne, like others in the movement, began peddling the line that Blair was nothing more than a subservient politician at Bush's beck and call.

In an article written in February 2002 titled, "Can the US be Defeated" he argues that Tony Blair lacks an independent spirit to distance himself from Bush: "Tony Blair has demonstrated none of the limited independence shown by earlier Labour ministers, such as Harold Wilson, and all the signs are that he will once again agree to whatever he is asked to on Britain's behalf."[33]

In September 2002 Milne wrote that what is "actually happening is that Blair, as Bush's senior international salesman is providing political cover for a policy which is opposed throughout the world." He concludes that for Blair, the Iraq war is about "his 'article of faith' in the centrality of the American relationship and the need to pay a 'blood price' to maintain it."[34]

On 21 November 2002 Milne refers to Blair as Bush's "faithful lieutenant."[35] Again, on the 16 January 2003 Blair is referred to as no more than a "salesman" for George W. Bush's anticipated war on Iraq.[36] But 2 weeks later, Blair is demoted to a mere "faithful cheerleader."[37]

Come February 2003, Milne cleverly turns the tables on the warmongers' fondness for associating Saddam with Hitler and therefore painting those who oppose war as nothing more than 1930s fascist appeasers. He argues it is rather Blair who is "appeasing" George W. Bush: "But if appeasement – unlike the form it took in the 1930s – is regarded as an attempt to pacify a powerful and potentially dangerous power, it sounds far more like the behaviour of Tony Blair's government towards the Bush administration."[38]

Just before the invasion of Iraq in March 2003, Donald Rumsfeld, the then American Defence Secretary, let it be known at a press conference that the United Kingdom's proposed role in the coming invasion was then inconclusive: "what will ultimately be decided is unclear as to their [Britain's] role in the event that a decision is made to use force." Speaking at the Pentagon, he added: "Until we know what the resolution is, we won't know what their role will be and the extent they'll be able to participate."[39]

In other words, Rumsfeld was openly saying that Britain can join the invasion if it wants to – basically the decision is theirs. This frank moment of honesty from one of the most high-level Bush officials exposed the false (anti-war) narrative peddled at the time about Blair being a "poodle," "cheerleader" or whatever subservient designation they saw befitting. In that brief moment, it was revealed that Blair was acting on his own accord in what he perceived to be the interests of the British establishment. This was later confirmed by Bob Woodward, the acclaimed American political author, in his book *Plan of Attack*. He records a conversation that took place between Bush and Blair:

"..Bush said he would let Blair drop out of the coalition and they would find some other way for Britain to participate.

"I said I'm with you. I mean it," Blair replied.

Bush said they could think of another role for the British forces – "a second wave, peacekeepers or something. I would rather go alone than have your government fail."

"I understand that," Blair responded, "and that's good of you to say. I said, I'm with you."

Bush said he really meant it that it would be okay for Blair to opt out. "You can bank on that."

"I know you do," Blair said, "and I appreciate that. I absolutely believe in this too.

"Thank you. I appreciate that. It's good of you to say that...
But I'm there to the very end.""[40]

Rumsfeld's candour and bluntness on Britain's potential role
threw Milne into panic and theatrics. He disingenuously asserted
that Tony Blair:

"had been stabbed in the back by the very US administration
for whom he had put his own leadership on the line. By
publicly calling into question Blair's ability to join a US
attack on Iraq, Donald Rumsfeld was clearly signalling the
Pentagon's impatience with the chaotic diplomatic quadrille
in New York and letting it be known that Blair's usefulness to
his US patrons may be close to being exhausted."[41]

Of course, no such "stab in the back" took place. Actually, it
was most likely Milne who felt betrayed because Rumsfeld had
totally undermined the central plank of his and the entire British
anti-war movement's argument for the reason why the UK was
joining the US in the invasion of Iraq. It was a war of Tony Blair's
own choosing.

On 10 April 2003, just after American tanks had rolled into
Baghdad, Milne was at it again claiming that "Blair is once again
seeking to provide a multilateral fig leaf for a policy set by
Washington hardliners."[42]

Many years later, Milne allowed himself to safely revert to
the essential truth about Blair. In February 2008, after Iraq had
then been almost forgotten and it was far from people's concerns,
Milne was able to write (referring to the aforementioned Blair
Chicago address) that during the NATO bombing campaign
over Kosovo: "Blair set out five tests for intervention as part
of his 'doctrine of international community', a catechism for
liberal interventionists much admired by the Washington
neoconservatives who followed them. Arguably, only one of the

five was met in Iraq."[43]

More so, former South African president Thabo Mbeki has claimed that Blair vouched the idea of a joint invasion of Zimbabwe in a regime-change operation.[44]

As can be easily discerned, Britain has led the way in insisting on war on Libya, Syria and indeed (alongside the US), Iraq.

As a side note, in March 2001, 6 months before the 9/11 attacks, a certain foreign adviser to Tony Blair sent him a memo advocating regime change in Iraq.[45] In the early stages of the US-UK occupation of Iraq, this same adviser became the UK government's Special Representative in Iraq. By 2009 he had begun his 5-year spell as head of the British intelligence agency MI6. By 2015, he was sitting comfortably on the roost of his 2001 memo; Sir John Sawers is now non-executive director of BP (formerly British Petroleum).[46]

The whole point of this short book is to put forward a modest yet empirically qualifiable case against one of the greatest political myths of the last 50 years, that is the notion that Britain is "America's poodle" and as such participates in wars out of some peculiar attachment to the United States or because of a misguided, one-sided friendship with the United States.

Therefore, I shall begin by covering the origins of England's foreign policy in piracy during Elizabeth Tudor's era in the following chapter. In the third chapter, I shall provide an overview, via British imperialist rule in India, which connects the piratical origins of this foreign policy with the unspoken British imperial presence in today's Persian Gulf. The forth chapter will detail how and why the United States and the British Empire ended up as allies especially as the Republic considered the Empire to be its nemesis for most of its existence before the twentieth century. The fifth chapter is in 3 sections. The first section is an overview of British imperialism's entry into the Arab World (or the 'Middle East' as it more popularly known in the UK) via World War One and specifically how British military defeats in Europe and Iraq compelled the Empire to make false promises to Arab leaders in support of its war efforts. Secondly, a conclusive outline on how Britain laid the foundations for the ethnic cleansing of Palestine by its proxy Zionist forces by crushing Palestinian requests for democracy. The third section is on how the Saudi clan came to power and were made into a nation-state (Kingdom of Saudi Arabia) to complement British imperialism and its Zionist project in Palestine. The information in the sections of the fourth chapter do overlap as the history in this period overlaps. I have tried to minimise any inevitable repetition. The sixth chapter deals with the notion of Britain as "America's poodle" within the historical period the derogation emerged, namely the Cold War between the United States and the Soviet Union.

Chapter 2

Origins of Contemporary British Imperialist Foreign Policy

"The discovery of gold and silver in America, the extirpation, enslavement and entombment in mines of the aboriginal population, the beginning of the conquest and looting of the East Indies, the turning of Africa into a warren for the commercial hunting of black-skins, signalised the rosy dawn of the era of capitalist production. These idyllic proceedings are the chief momenta of primitive accumulation."
Karl Marx

"The voyages I planned is to lade Negroes in Guinea and sell them in the West Indies in truck, gold, pearls and emeralds, whereof I doubt not but to bring home great abundance to the contention of your highness and to the relief of the number of worthy servitures..."
John Hawkins to Queen Elizabeth Tudor (aka Elizabeth I)

Only after the British public voted to leave the European Union, and specifically after the process to actually leave was triggered many months later, was it acknowledged by commentators in the mainstream media that post-World War Two British history has been re-written. Post 1945, the mainstream British story became one of a stalwart liberal democracy which stood alone in the face of Hitler Germany's brutal expansionism. As the multi-million book selling science author, ex-banker and journalist Matt Ridley argued, in the immediate post-war period Britain basically turned its back on its imperialist record and "rewrote its story as that of a plucky underdog standing up to the Nazi bully."[1]

That the British had an empire which in practice inflicted just as much blood-soaked pain on the people of Africa, Asia and elsewhere as Adolf Hitler did and intended more to do on Europe is an anathema and taboo subject to this day. That the British establishment, which had hitherto prided itself on its racial superiority and the imperial conquest of a healthy geographical proportion of planet earth before 1939, was compelled to beg for assistance from its former colony, the United States of America, to rescue it from Germany's version of racial superiority and conquest, is not a proposition that will endear itself to the overwhelming majority of subjects of this supposed United Kingdom. Gideon Rachman, the *Financial Times* commentator and former editor of *The Economist*, wrote that: "the most interesting thing about modern British history would surely be that the country built a massive global empire. But for the Brits themselves, shaping a national story that centres around the war against the Nazis...makes psychological sense. It has allowed Britain to nurture a national self-image as champions of freedom and plucky underdogs...rather than imperialist oppressors."[2]

It is only in this context of "nurturing" and "rewriting" or what impartial people would refer to as brainwashing, if we were to speak of a disagreeable country, that one can appreciate the success of Professor Niall Fergusons's celebration of British imperialism in his popular book, *Empire: How Britain Made the Modern World*. Herein, he acknowledges that in contrast to the United States of America, Great Britain in its heyday was "able to draw on a culture of unabashed imperialism" rooted in the Elizabethan period.[3] Queen Elizabeth Tudor or Elizabeth I ruled England between 1558 and 1603.

The aim of this chapter is to outline how contemporary British imperialist foreign policy towards the people of Africa and Asia began in the late sixteenth century. It will show how a particular method employed by leading Elizabethan seafarers provided the springboard for English foreign adventurism to fork off in two directions, trade in Asia and colonialism in the western hemisphere.

The Tudors had originally established themselves as rulers of England and Wales in 1485 when Henry VII militarily defeated Richard III. Upon Henry VII's death in 1509, his son Henry VIII succeeded to the throne. The latter Henry, upon being denied a divorce by the Pope, decided to divorce the English Church from Rome.

He acrimoniously consolidated the separation from Rome by plundering what had once been Rome's possessions in England or "had a great part enriched [England's]...crown with Dissolution of the Monastries, pillaging Church treasures and Church lands for himself and his cronies."[4] David Childs, a writer on the supposed "foundation of greatness" of British imperialism, confirms that: "it is difficult to see in the split from Rome and the dissolution of the monasteries any motive more dominant that the king's concern with sex, supremacy and the succession, and his lust for the wealth of others."[5]

Elizabeth I, one of Henry VIII's children, acceded to the throne in 1558 and so began the Elizabethan era. But Ferguson is not the only historian who has pinpointed the Elizabethan period as seminal in paving a new direction for English foreign policy. Kenneth Andrews, in his study *Trade, Plunder and Settlement,* claims the Elizabethan crown "led the forces of the nation in the plunder of Iberian shipping"[6] and according to the historian Susan Roland, it was this roguish brand of internationalism that heralded "a new force in English foreign policy."[7]

The "force" in question is nothing mysterious or ethereal that only the spiritually elect can comprehend. The force in question is piracy. That is, extortion on the seas. Basically, preying on ships on the seas was in effect banditry or highwaymen taken to the seas.[8]

Piracy is not new in human history. For example, Professor Noam Chomsky recounts St Augustine's story of an encounter between Alexander the Great and a captured pirate. Alexander berates the pirate for preying on the seas but the pirate replies that because he does "it with a little ship only, I am called a thief; you, doing it with a great navy, are called an Emperor."[9]

Before Elizabethan piracy, England's major trade was in cloth. The main product it exchanged with the world was unfinished wool and some grain. But, as Childs states, English traders found that in: "the open ocean, or in distant ports,…[one] could obtain the same goods merely for the price of some powder and shot and loss of some seamen, all of which came cheap."[10]

From the other end of the barrel, for a so-called "seaman" in the sixteenth century, adventurism on the seas was a way to potentially ameliorate poverty and harsh material circumstances. According to Andrews, piracy "grew spontaneously out of poverty and unemployment among seamen."[11] What was then looted at sea was brought back to England's shores and traded. Therefore, piracy is not rooted in an ideal or a romance but in existence. Desperate people needed an income and piracy was one way of obtaining that income. The booty brought in by pirates complemented the season's harvest. But if the harvest fell short, for whatever reason, the maritime booty was what allowed life to continue.[12]

Furthermore, as Ronald argues in her thesis, "Maritime theft had become more than a national pastime that neatly exported penniless rogues and thieves away from the towns and cities," because when these "adventurers" returned they not only became less of a threat to their fellow subjects as they had already made their livelihood being twistedly entrepreneurial on the seas, more so, they became ideals or heroes spawning other "adventurers."[13] Another historian has argued that pirates were not condemned but tolerated as long as English shipping was not in their crosshairs because their fruits "provided a stream of cheap goods for local toughs who might otherwise have been engaged in robbing their neighbours."[14] In other words, let the pirate rob Johnny Foreigner out on the seas and out of view rather than preying on his own kith and kin.

Initially pirates unleashed themselves on what is now called the English Channel. English and French pirates made their reputations by preying on Iberian and Netherlands shipping which by the end of 1563, a mere 5 years after Elizabeth came to power, had cost the latter two the equivalent of £6.27 billion in today's currency.[15]

In the mid-1560s English pirates spread their wings and began to target Spanish and Portuguese shipping. Rome had divided the so-called new world between the two Iberian powers, Spain and Portugal. As Ferguson writes, in "1493 the Pope had issued a bull allocating trade in the Americas to Spain and trade in Asia to Portugal. In this division of the world, the Portuguese had got the sugar, spices and slaves."[16] In this economic order only the Portuguese were allowed to do business with the new Spanish colonies in South America and it was into this papal division of the world that Elizabethan pirates interloped and made their name.

The most consequential English pirates during this period are John Hawkins, Francis Drake and Walter Raleigh. Their expeditions and strategies founded and defined an era with reverberations to this day.

John Hawkins (1532-95) established his piratical credentials and value to the Elizabethan regime with four expeditions in the 1560s. His intentions on these voyages were firmly expressed in a letter approvingly received by the Queen: "The voyages I planned is to lade Negroes in Guinea and sell them in the West Indies in truck, gold, pearls and emeralds, whereof I doubt not but to bring home great abundance to the contention of your highness and to the relief of the number of worthy servitures..."[17]

Arguably this is the foundational modus operandi of what underpins the so-called "unabashed imperialism" Ferguson has in mind and the "worthy servitures" are no doubt a reference to the individual investors in these voyages. "Guinea" was the given European name for most of what is now west Africa.

Hawkins was England's first state sanctioned "trader" in captured, kidnapped and enslaved Africans. His method was to voyage to the west African coast and raid Portuguese ships, looting the goods and stealing already captured Africans. If the possessions from the shipping raids fell short, he and his crew ventured inland to raid, kidnap and capture Africans.[18] In their incursions inland Hawkins's chronicler noted the superior level of African civilisation. At a time when Plymouth "was little more than sewer" and London was a "hovel astride the Thames" Africans had order, high quality craftsmanship and their settlements were organised into what today are referred to as standard towns with a central square. On certain occasions the leaders would assemble to discuss and agree the major issues affecting the settlement.[19]

Once his ships were loaded with cargo and shackled Africans, Hawkins would proceed to Spain's South American colonies and aggressively sell his booty or "trade" with mainly Spanish colonialists. Upon arriving at his destination, he would parlay to be excused of his presence at their settlements but he and his crew were mere victims of inclement weather conditions which randomly brought them forth to these shores with captured Africans to sell.[20] He had set out on his first voyage in October 1562 and returned with his illicit profits in September 1563.

This formula of setting out to sail for west Africa, capturing Africans, aggressive trade in South America and then returning with illicit rewards was the template for all four of Hawkins's voyages in the 1560s bar the third, which although financed by Hawkins was led by an employee.

The most significant voyage was the second in October 1564, when he secured the Queen's overt support to borrow her "Jesus of Lubeck" ship. By providing him with a ship, Elizabeth I was openly investing and endorsing this slave expedition.[21] The ship "bristled with heavy bronze and iron artillery. As the admiral of the fleet, it had the sort of devastating firepower that befitted a royal Tudor floating fortress."[22] Like the first voyage, Hawkins once again set out for the west African coast. There he attacked and robbed Portuguese fishermen and plundered Portuguese shipping and took hold of already captured Africans. According to the Portuguese, Hawkins and his fellow pirates stole "wax, gold, ivory and at least sixty slaves from Sierra Leone."[23] He then set sail for South America to sell his loot. Once again, he informed the Spanish colonialists that inclement weather conditions had thrown him "off course" but, lo and behold, he had cargo that might be of interest to them.[24] He returned to Cornwall, England in September 1565.

The gruesome highlight of his final expedition was when he traded with the South American Spanish settlement of Rio de la Hacha. He achieved commercial success with the local inhabitants "by dint of burning part of the town and beginning to make off with some of the citizens and quantities of pillage that he finally brought the local government to heel."[25] In the twentieth century such a strategy gained iconic and popular currency with the film adaption of Mario Puzo's The Godfather. The lead character, a certain Mr Vito Corleone, would apply the threat of physical force to compel his business rivals to appreciate "an offer they couldn't refuse." Hawkins's method of negotiation in South America during the Elizabethan era was no different.

It needs to be emphasised that the booty brought back by Hawkins and other pirates to England's harbours greatly assisted in ameliorating the effects of poor harvests, poverty and general socio-economic tensions. In effect this treasure was at times the difference between "starvation and survival."[26] Hawkins's voyages changed England and in later years "their goals would become ever more commercial" and colonial, to the extent that they "would fundamentally change the very fabric of English society."[27]

Unsurprisingly, Hawkins became a national hero and the Queen bestowed on him a knighthood.[28] This inspired other pirates such as Francis Drake to go it alone in search of treasure for Queen and country.[29]

Francis Drake had distinguished himself on Hawkins's latter voyages as a master seaman. It was during the 1570s, however, that he etched his own reputation. Born into criminality through a father who was a highway robber baron and a thief,[30] Drake cast aside the state sanctioned veneer of voyaging to west Africa on so-called "trade" expeditions. He simply cut to the chase and voyaged to the Caribbean and Spain's South American colonies and tirelessly but joyously plundered the Spanish and Portuguese or as one of Drake's biographers writes: "Drake merely took the process further."[31]

Spain had become the main imperial power in the sixteenth century largely due to its exploitation of South America and specifically the exploitation of the gold and silver mines of that continent.

In 1571, Drake targeted the trade route bringing ships from Central America to Spain. His focus was on attacking the isthmus, the narrow strip of land linking South and North America. He raided and looted at least 12 ships belonging to both Spain and Portugal. The loot he returned to England with would be valued at £14.58 million in today's money, more than the combined amount Hawkins had brought back on three of his voyages.[32]

By July 1572 he had departed again but with a specific focus on the Spanish safe houses or the treasure houses. These houses hoarded the gold and silver upon its arrival from the South American heartland before it was loaded onto ships bound for Spain. One of the main treasure houses was the town called Nombre de Dios which Drake and his men successfully captured by attacking it in the early hours of the morning as its inhabitants slept. However, this successful raid was short lived as Drake and his men needed to retreat due to the former's battle injury.[33] With the Spanish now alerted to his presence, Drake needed to alter his strategy in order to capture any treasure. Teaming up with escaped Africans they decided to wait and attack the treasure as it was en route to the treasure houses from South America.[34]

In the intervening months, while waiting for the treasure to arrive, Drake and his gang pre-occupied themselves with plundering and pillaging shipping on the coast of the isthmus.[35] His patience was eventually rewarded in March 1573, when Drake and his men attacked the treasure chain as it was being hauled on about 200 heavily laden animals. The booty seized by Drake totalled £19.22 million.[36] Drake returned to England a hero.[37]

What followed this successful piratical escapade for Drake, was a lull – a pirate's sabbatical, of a sort. The Elizabethan regime despatched him to Ireland to assist in the oppression and occupation of the Irish. The unabashed highlight of his time during this stint was the massacre of the inhabitants of Rathlin Island.

In 1576, one of Elizabeth Tudor's closest advisers, John Dee, published a paper, "A Petty Naval Royal" which proposed an outline for the future course for the defence of England. Central to this proposal was ship building and maintaining a standing navy on England's shores. He invoked the notion of a "British Empire" for possibly the first time in England's history.[38] Dee also suggested that one of the positive aspects of the English regime building more ships would be the amelioration of social issues such as crime, vagrancy and idleness: "How many hundreds of lusty and handsome men would be, this way well occupied, and have needful maintenance, which now are either idle, or want sustenance, or both…"[39]

If one were to draw a twentieth century parallel with Dee's line of thinking, the notion that the state "investing" in its maritime military capabilities will also generate employment to its people is known as "Military Keynesianism." That is, the idea that state spending on improving its military prowess provides "needful maintenance" for the kingdom's subjects can be traced back to the Elizabethan era.

Upon returning from Ireland, Drake set sail for his next expedition to South America. His squadron of five ships, the *Elizabeth, Pelican, Swan, Marigold* and *Christopher*, set out in December 1577. By the time he reached the Cape Verde Islands he had already captured and plundered (or "held up the old English traditions"[40]) another ship which he lovingly renamed *Mary*, after, who else, his wife.

Unlike his first mission which targeted the isthmus or the second which had targeted the safe houses, this third piratical mission was to cleverly target shipping on the western coastline of South America.

In August 1578, he finally arrived close to what was then thought to be the southern most point of the South American coast, the Strait of Magellan. Journeying through the strait would allow him to reach his intended target. At this point, he had already lost three ships due to turbulent weather conditions crossing the Atlantic Ocean. The *Elizabeth, Pelican* and *Marigold* survived. Herein, for some unknown reason, Drake renamed the *Pelican*, the *Golden Hind*.[41]

As he travelled through the Strait of Magellan, the *Marigold* was lost due to heavy winds and the Elizabeth, having lost sight and touch with the *Golden Hind*, turned back and returned to England. Drake on the other hand persevered and finally exited the strait in September 1578 but then a heavy wind blew them back south, and it was then inadvertently "discovered" that the Strait of Magellan was not the furthest point in South America as hitherto had been believed.[42]

Upon regaining his compass, Drake could now focus on his mission which "was to plunder the western coast of Spanish America and to bring the treasure back to England"[43] or as Andrews expressed it, he "turned his attention fully and doubtless cheerfully to that unofficial business his promoters expected him to tract – the 'making' of the voyage."[44]

Travelling north up the western coast of South America, Drake captured an indigenous person in a canoe who was cajoled into assisting with the navigation. They eventually reached a port called Valparaiso wherein Drake and his men ransacked it "in an orgy of looting."[45]

Drake's success in plundering ships on the pacific side of South America was based on the fact that no non-Spanish ship had ever been to this part of the continent. Therefore, the element of surprise was always on his side because no one assumed his ship to be anything other than a Spanish one or at least a friendly ship. By March 1579, Drake had plundered and captured treasures to the tune of £3.66 million.[46]

In March 1579 Drake hit the pirate's jackpot. He captured a Spanish ship called the *Nuestra Senora de la Concepcion* which added a further £26.82 million of treasure to his already hard-earned burgeoning pillage.[47] No Englishman before Drake had ever stolen so much from the Spanish and his major concern after this haul was how best to return to England. He continued to travel north along the coast in search of a mythical north American strait which was hoped would take him back through to northern Europe.[48] This north American strait was supposedly a short cut back to Europe which bypassed Spanish territory. In doing so, he also took advantage of the lack of defences on certain ports such as what is today the Mexican port of Guatulco which he ransacked and plundered in April 1579.[49]

The mythical northern strait did not materialise as commonly assumed by the English regime. He realised that he could not return the way he arrived because the Spanish were blatantly aware of his presence on the western coast of Spanish America or as Andrews states the "Spaniards were fully alerted."[50] He had no choice but to opt for the safest route back to England which was via the Pacific Ocean and by default become the first

Englishman to circumnavigate the world if he was to avoid capture by the Spanish.[51]

By September 1579, he had reached Micronesia but left quickly after getting embroiled in skirmishes with local inhabitants. Elizabeth's maritime gangsters then moved onto the spice islands of Ternate and Java where the Portuguese had already established trade links. Brisk trade was conducted and he set out into the Indian Ocean in March 1580, arriving at Cape Good Hope in June and finally Plymouth on 26 September 1580.[52]

Within a year of his return to England he was ceremoniously knighted on the Golden Hind in London to cheering crowds. The looter, plunderer, pillager, ransacker and future Parliamentarian became Sir Francis Drake. After all, the Queen was always grateful to the likes of Drake and her other pirates because their enterprises provided her "with a considerable war chest."[53] But specifically she had much to be grateful for, her government's share from Drake's *Golden Hind* booty wiped out England's national debt.

Drake's maritime "success" rippled through and inspired all levels of English society. On one level according to Andrews, Drake symbolised and embodied the "social aspirations of the masses."[54] For "gentlemen-adventurers" Drake inspired them in the "pursuit of gold and glory beyond the straits."[55] In both instances Drake's murderous pillaging and plundering expedition inflated "the national ego, helping more than any other single achievement to create a new mood of confidence in maritime adventure. It...stimulated the extraordinary proliferation of projects for trade, plunder and colonisation that marked the period from 1578 to 1584."[56] And one could argue well beyond 1584 and to this very day.

It is close to certain that the legacy of another Elizabethan pirate, Walter Raleigh, owes much to the death of his half-brother, Humphrey Gilbert.

As a military captain in Ireland, Gilbert had "delighted in

inflicting massive causalities in as vile a manner as possible. Deliberately killing as many women and children...[but]his particular speciality was to lay waste to the land, cut off his victim's heads, and use them as markers forming a gruesome path to his tent."[57] While terrorising and crushing the Irish, Gilbert had also been witness to England's attempts to forcefully anglicise the country with English settlements. This inspired him to gain royal approval and the patent for colonial settlement in North America.

In September 1583, Gilbert disappeared with his ship as it sank on a return journey from North America. Walter Raleigh very quickly picked up his half-brother's mantel and the royal patent to establish colonial settlements. He set out on his first North American mission in 1584, the second in 1585. The first was a reconnaissance mission, the latter an actual settlement mission headed by a certain Ralph Lane. Raleigh didn't go because it is said the Queen wanted him close at hand as the clouds of war with Spain were gathering.

The purpose of the new settlement enterprise was firstly as a pirate base to attack and plunder Spanish shipping as they set off from the West Indies back to Spain and secondly as an agricultural plantation to supply England with foodstuffs. As such, the new settlement could potentially act as an outlet for England's "surplus poor."[58] That is, surplus labour could be sent to the new colony rather than being idle and mischievous in England.

Unlike Hawkins and Drake, Raleigh was also an intellectual promoter of building a British Empire at the expense of Spanish imperialism. As such he advocated a particular strategy that is all too familiar today. He believed in undermining Spanish rule in central and southern America by championing the cause of the indigenous population who had suffered terribly under Spain. Raleigh wanted to manipulate their suffering and hopes and make allies of them to further the interests of the Elizabethan regime.[59] Like the modern Western humanitarian interventionist who solely focuses on the wrongs of official enemies, Raleigh too was totally inconsistent in his approach to humanitarianism. His actual participation in the slaughter of the Irish resistance against English rule in Smerwick in 1580 exposes his concern for the indigenous population of southern and central America as cruel expediency.

However, the first attempts at English colonisation in North America ended in failure largely because there was no short-term gain from colonisation, whereas piracy reaped immediate benefits.

Noting England's ambitions and its meddling in internecine warfare elsewhere on the European mainland between Catholics and Protestants, the Pope issued a directive (or a papal bull) to finish off the "heretical state" of England.[60] Imperial Spain sent its Armada which failed to invade England on more than one occasion. In turn, the Elizabethan regime issued "letters of reprisals" to its own seamen who felt wronged by Spain confiscating their trade ships. Many of these letters of reprisals were seemingly fraudulent. As Andrews argues, quite inevitably, "proof of losses became little more than a legal fiction, and reprisals were promoted by men who had never dreamed of trading in Spain."[61] Roland corroborates this deception and claims that it was a certain Sir Julius who was employed at the High Court of the Admiralty who "issued the letters of reprisal, often accepting fiction as fact."[62] The conjuring of trade grievances against Imperial Spain manifesting in letters of reprisal provided a legal pretext to attack and ransack Spanish shipping for the next 18 years of intermittent war with Spain.

On this basis, it is no surprise that England's colonisation of North America and the Caribbean only began to flourish after peace with Spain was established in 1604. Just as importantly, the financiers who led the way in the sea war against Spain were one and the same that launched the East India Company, that ultimately came to rule India. Kenneth Andrews identifies businessmen such as Thomas Cordell, James Lancaster, Thomas Allabaster and Paul Bayning, who all made their money in the war with Spain, as among the organisers behind the committee that drove the first expedition of the East India Company (EIC). Three of the four ships that made the EIC's first trading voyage began their merchantry as "privateering" ships in the Spanish war.[63]

Some historians have kindly drawn a distinction between pirates and privateers with a view to disassociating the state from naked maritime theft. But the very term "privateering" only came into parlance in the eighteenth century.[64]

As for the Caribbean colonies, St Christopher was acquired in 1624, followed by Barbados in 1627. Jamaica was captured from Imperial Spain in 1655. These colonies as well as the newly established settlements in North America required labour for the plantations which grew tobacco, sugar, cotton and other crops. The source of this labour was fulfilled by emulating the Portuguese in capturing, chaining and shipping Africans from the west coast of Africa in their millions to the western hemisphere.

The British eventually became the largest traders in captured Africans (i.e "slave trade") after gaining an asiento to supply the Spanish colonies in the Treaty of Utrecht in 1713, almost 66 years after the union of England and Scotland which produced the new "Great Britain."

The development of these western colonies and settlements with enslaved Africans provided all sections of British society with its fabulous wealth. As Eric Williams argued in his book, *Capitalism and Slavery*, before 1783 "all classes in English society presented a united front with regard to the slave trade. The monarchy, the government, the church, public opinion in general supported the slave trade."[65] The British historian David Olusoga, commenting on recent research on the slave trade, states that slave ownership "was far more common than has been previously presumed." It was not just the aristocracy or the wealthy but also "bit-players" such as vicars, iron manufacturers and lots and lots of widows." Most importantly, "Slavery was once thought of as an activity largely limited to the ports from which the ships of the triangular trade set sail; Bristol, London, Liverpool and Glasgow. Yet there were slave owners across the country, from Cornwall to the Orkneys."[66] Piracy not only laid the foundations of an imperialist foreign policy, but was also the nucleus of an imperialist people.

The triangular trade in question involved products from England which were taken to west Africa, traded for captured Africans who were then transported to the western colonies to work as slaves on the European settlements and plantations. The produce of these plantations was then exported to the United Kingdom and other European countries.

Furthermore, the cruel and blood-soaked profits accrued by the British Empire and its metropolitan populace from the triangular trade with the colonies provided the finances and investments which fabulously fuelled Britain's industrial revolution.[67]

The impact of Francis Drake's legacy reverberates to the modern era. Margaret Thatcher evoked Drake's supposed values in the late 1980s when she was going through a difficult patch. Paraphrasing the pirate's alleged prayer (apparently to God) she said that, "When you have set your hand to any great endeavour, it is not the beginning but the continuation of the same until it be well and truly finished…"[68] One of the ships currently under construction by the British Navy is named after a ship Drake commandeered and sailed on during the years of war with Imperial Spain.

From the very inception of English and then British foreign policy we can determine fundamental themes which continue to be extant to this very day such as the export of surplus population to newly acquired territory; manufacturing consent for foreign adventurism on the basis of humanitarian concerns for its population at the hands of their current rulers; public funds for military expenditure which in turn provides employment to a populace that otherwise would be unemployed and indeed, potentially troublesome; false pretexts to wage wars of aggression and the acquiescence, if not celebration, of the domestic metropolis in imperialist military adventurism. Some of these themes re-occur throughout this short study.

So when we hear right-wing British nationalist or today's Brexit supporters declare that Britain has always been a "maritime nation," it is important to remind ourselves that when unpacked and clarified the very actual notion of "maritime nation" is indefatigably and irrefutably rooted in piracy or theft on the high seas. On the other hand, when we read today's leaders of the British anti-war movement (Stop the War Coalition), Andrew Murray and Chris Nineham, correctly state that war "has been a more-or-less constant since the [American] Republic's foundation," they may want to entertain the notion that the British too have been at war with mankind not only since its foundation, but since the founding of the modern English regime in the Elizabethan era.[69]

Chapter 3

From Piracy to Indirect Rule via the Pillage of India

"I read how, entering India – half a billion deeply religious brown people – the British white man by 1759, through promises, trickery and manipulations, controlled much of India through Great Britain's East India Company. The parasitical British administration kept tentacling out to half of the sub-continent. In 1857, some of the desperate people of India finally mutinied – and expecting the African slave trade, nowhere has history recorded any more unnecessary bestial and ruthless human carnage that the British suppression of the non-white Indian people."[1]
Malcolm X

This chapter establishes a connection between the end of the piracy period, the conquest of India and how the imperialist strategy used to consolidate British rule in India after the great Indian uprising in 1857 can be seen employed in today's Persian Gulf where British interests are paramount.

The wealth accrued from piracy and war on Spanish and Portuguese shipping allowed England's establishment to follow in the rapacious path of these then imperial hegemons. As the famous economist Adam Smith had written, "The discovery of America, and that of a passage to the East Indies by the Cape of Good Hope are the two greatest and most important events recorded in the history of mankind."[2] In truth there was no so-called "discovery" of America but simply and cruelly European wars of annihilation of the indigenous populations, first in South America and then in North America with Caribbean Islands in between.

The other "discovery," that is, of a passage to Asia via the

Cape of Good Hope, allowed Europeans to bypass the traditional land route for goods through what is now called the "Middle East" and specifically Aleppo. Travelling directly by sea to the source of spices and other Asian goods allowed European adventurers to cut out the multiple middlemen one inevitably encountered on land. On this basis, the English Crown bestowed upon the English EIC a guaranteed monopoly on all trade between England and the world beyond the Cape of Good Hope, which is on the most southern tip of Africa, in 1600. As such, the EIC managed to reduce prices by up to two-thirds.[3] It would be an insult to history to insist this remarkable reduction of prices in the early years of the EIC was achieved solely by trade, as the historian Nick Robins grudgingly admits: "Pirates have an ambiguous place in English folklore...the first wave of East India traders simply continued an old English tradition: trade where necessary and plunder where possible."[4]

It is no surprise that one of the EIC's first representatives to India was a certain William Hawkins, nephew of John Hawkins, Queen Elizabeth's first major pirate.

Eventually, the EIC came to work out of four main ports in India: Surat, Bombay, Madras and Calcutta, importing spices and textiles to the home market. After decades of trading in Asia the EIC made its first land grab for Indian territory in the 1680s. One of the main reasons for this new strategy was that if the EIC became sovereign over Indian land it would financially absolve itself of the need to pay any duties on its imports and exports to Indian authorities. The EIC's then director, Josiah Child in England, sent instructions to the EIC's council in Madras to establish a base for a civil and military power there with a view to dominating India forever.[5] The expeditionary mission he despatched was defeated by Mughal emperor Aurangzeb.

Surprisingly, the EIC was allowed to continue trading on the basis that India's rulers had sole authority to impose regulations on all trade and as such the EIC was subject to the same duties on imports and exports as other traders, be they Indian or European.

In 1716 Emperor Farrukhsiyar granted the EIC an imperial licence to duty-free trade in three provinces, Bengal, Hyderabad and Ahmedabad. The licence also authorised the EIC to issue dastaks (i.e. passes) which exempted certain shipments from paying duties. In the Bengal, the EIC took advantage of this authorisation and began issuing passes to inland traders as well as other exporters denying essential revenue to the Emperor's deputy, the Nawab, in that province. Finally, the issue came to a head in the 1750s. The passing away of Nawab Ali Vardi led to the accession of Siraj al-Dawlah who seemed determined to put an end to EIC excesses and abuses. Among the excesses which had aggravated him and his predecessor was the increasing militarisation of Fort William within the English settlement in Bengal.

Tensions rose between the new Nawab and the EIC but the straw that finally broke the camel's back was when an employee of Siraj al-Dawlah successfully sought refuge at the English settlement after falling out with him. British refusal to extradite him compelled the Nawab to take decisive action against the EIC.[6] The Nawab began his military campaign in late May 1756 and by the end of the following month the British surrendered their settlement and fort.[7]

On the same evening of the surrender some disruptive Europeans who had fought with the British, apparently under the influence of liquor, were held in a "Black Hole" within the fort.[8]

The Nawab's victory proved to be short lived. Most of the British forces had simply retreated whereby once re-organised, replenished and reinforced they cunningly concocted a conspiracy to not only avenge the defeat and reclaim their settlement but to occupy Bengal entirely. The EIC decided in September 1756 against any kind of compromise with the Nawab as they knew that if one was reached it would be on the Nawab's terms.[9] Another factor that clearly must have influenced the EIC's decision for war was that it was commercially performing badly when compared to other Asian and European traders.[10] To respectively continue as a profitable company it had no choice but to conspire a winner-takes-all war on the Nawab otherwise the competition may have financially destroyed the company.

The conspiracy's success rested on employees of the Nawab accepting a bribe from Britain's Colonel Robert Clive to defect in war once it finally occurred at the Battle of Plassey in June 1757. The forces of the EIC with their Indian traitors defeated the Nawab and became victorious over the Bengal region of India.[11]

When news of the Plassey victory finally reached England it was reported that Clive's war was in retribution for European prisoner deaths in the "Black Hole" of Calcutta. This was the main false pretext provided to justify the EIC's war, occupation and rule of Bengal. This victory for the company also provided it with a foothold and springboard for the eventual political, military and economic hegemony over India entirely.[12]

Before Plassey, the Indian "sub-continent" accounted for almost a quarter of global manufacturing.[13] Bengal alone had supplied the EIC with 66 per cent of its goods by 1740. But even this doesn't provide a true picture of how comparatively affluent Bengal was compared to the rest of the world because Bengal's trade with all Europeans only amounted to a third of its total exports, the rest of the trade was with other Asian dominions.[14] Moreover, the EIC in the first decades of the eighteenth century leading to Plassey traded with mostly silver-bullion no doubt obtained from Spain in return for enslaved Africans.[15]

As Robins has argued in his account of the EIC, *The Corporation that Changed the World*, the "honourable company" (as it was nicknamed) had not only subdued a dynasty but in effect had defeated the commercial regulatory powers of Bengal as personified by the Nawab. They then literally and piratically helped themselves to the wealth of Bengal and looted the region to their heart's content.

One of the first entities to feel the lash of the new British order in Bengal were French and other European competition who were inevitably made persona non grata, i.e. thrown out.[16] No more European competition meant the EIC literally had Bengal to itself and that meant the Bengal worker was to suffer horrendously because all bargaining was removed. Once the British were the sole rulers, the Bengali workforce no longer had any negotiating rights because they had to settle for the price dictated to them by the EIC. The Indian producer had no one else to trade with besides the EIC and its servants.

More so, before the battle at Plassey, the EIC "simply did not have the skills or capacity to buy goods direct from the producers" so another cost was eliminated with the military victory.[17] With this in mind, it is no surprise that there were reports of Bengali weavers choosing to cut off their thumbs rather than work under the new British despotism.[18] The British imperialists literally pauperised the Bengali workforce by oppressing them, the ramifications of which remain to this very day.[19]

On a personal level, in the immediate aftermath of the victory at Plassey, Clive pocketed £24.5 million, while earning a "windfall" of £262 million for the EIC in today's money.[20] On the other hand, Nawab Siraj ud-Dawlah was immediately executed. The new puppet Nawab Mir Jafar, who had conspired with Clive, was installed in July 1757. Later in 1760, the EIC replaced Jafar with his son-in-law, Mir Kasim. Come 1763, Kasim had proven himself to be too independently minded and wanted to bring to an end the impoverishment of the Bengali worker. One of the puppet's complaints was that the EIC's own paid agents, gomastas, had replaced the need for Indian middlemen. These gomastas who seemed to be the then business thugs of the EIC, helped themselves to the goods of the Bengali producer for a quarter of their value and forced a value of goods on the producer five times their worth.[21]

As a result of disillusionment with the EIC rule, Mir Kasim entered an alliance with another Nawab (in the Awadh region of India) as well as the forces of the Mughal emperor Shah Alam II in battle against the forces of the EIC at Buxor in October 1764. But once again, the EIC proved victorious. The previously deposed puppet Mir Jafar was returned as Nawab for the final months of his life, before the company installed his son as the new token ruler of Bengal in early 1765.[22]

Magnificently for the EIC, by August 1765 not only did it have a total business monopoly over Bengal and its surrounding areas, it was also "granted" diwani rights for the entire region by the Mughal emperor which meant that it had tax collection raising rights over 20 million people added to its balance sheets.[23]

Grabbing hold of the Bengali diwani allowed the EIC then to expand into the Chinese tea trade and also help the British government to pay off debts left behind from the 7-year war with France.[24] Indeed, there was no longer any need for the EIC to send bullion from London to pay for Bengal goods as the EIC now had authority over the diwani.

The years 1757 to 1764, that is the years between the battles of Plassey and Buxor, were not only the foundations of British imperial rule in India but on the flip-side the foundations of Indian impoverishment. British dominance inaugurated a new era of regular famines. One historian in the late-nineteenth century had written that in the 120 years of British rule in India there had been 34 famines, while only 17 were recorded in the previous 2000 years.[25] The first to afflict Bengal was not surprisingly soon after the EIC established dominance over it.[26] In 1770, as millions of Bengalis were literally starving to death, EIC officials laughed off complaints that they were hoarding rice. As Robins wrote, "Huge fortunes were made" as EIC officials cornered the rice market and Indians perished in their millions.[27]

Bengal became the principle template as the EIC militarily

expanded across the Indian sub-continent. India was to be impoverished along Bengal lines with the EIC helping itself to the wealth of the new territories it continuously acquired.

Upon entering a new area (or kingdom) in India, the EIC would appoint "Residents" to sit in the courts of native rulers, be it a Nawab or Raja (titles of Indian rulers) to make sure the local ruler's policies were always to the advantage of the British.[28] In effect, the role of the Resident was to make sure the ruler governed with the EIC's insatiable interests in mind. This 'Residency' system, which allowed the EIC to rule over the nominal native ruler, came to be known as 'indirect rule' as opposed to obvious direct rule where a ruler is completely deposed and the EIC takes over the running of the area. Dr Michael Fisher in his study *Indirect Rule in India* defines it as: "the exercise of determinative and exclusive political control by one corporate body over a nominally sovereign state, a control recognised by both sides."[29]

Fisher argues that the main benefit of indirect rule was that it shielded the dominant power, i.e. the EIC, the actual ruling agency from the hostility of the populace. Therefore, if any anger at the policies instituted by the state brewed to the surface, it was hoped it would be directed against the surficial ruler rather than the true sovereign of the land.[30]

The dominance of the EIC was further guaranteed by a treaty with a subjugated ruler. The treaties always insisted that the Resident controlled the communication channels between the ruler's court and the company as well as with other rulers under EIC hegemony.[31] This arrangement helped the EIC to prevent rulers from different Indian states uniting against it. On the other hand, Residents posted in various parts of the sub-continent were allowed to communicate directly with each other at will.[32] Obviously, the aim of this arrangement was to divide and rule. As Fisher writes: "By careful negotiation, the Residents were to break up combinations of Indian states forming against the Company and further to ally Indian states with the Company against others hostile to them."[33]

Furthermore, to keep each ruler in a state of subjugation and subservience to the EIC, the latter insisted that the native ruler reduce military expenditure in his patch while at the same time compelling the ruler to subsidise the military forces at the Resident's immediate disposal. What was left of a ruler's own army was not allowed to be employed beyond his own patch as defined by the company.[34] In 1801, the Awadh ruler was required to cede half of its territory to the company in order to pay for the company's military presence in his territory.[35]

Originally, the system of indirect rule was the penultimate phase the EIC adopted over an Indian state before annexing the state outright. By annexing the territory of the Indian rulers, the EIC claimed the right to acquire revenue and taxes as well as the right to depose local rulers. Annexations could be justified on the basis that the local ruler was mismanaging and oppressing his people and his terrain was awash with corruption and "bad government."

On this basis, some Indian rulers were understandably very suspicious of the EIC appointing Residents and declined to host them but this only invited company wrath and war. Tipu Sultan was a leader who rejected the EIC's Resident but was later defeated in battle. Others that resisted EIC encroachment include the rulers of Travancore, Jaipur and Sind.[36] Overall, for one reason or another, the EIC had to fend off a total of 40 rebellions between 1760 and 1850.[37]

Between 1848 and 1856 the EIC intensified the annexation of Indian land to the tune of 250,000 square miles, which amounted to a quarter of its land holdings in the sub-continent.[38] A region called Sattara was annexed in 1848; Nagpur was annexed in 1853. The Punjab, which was under the nominal rulership of Dalip Singh, was annexed in 1849 on the basis that he was conspiring against the EIC with Afghan rulers[39] (as we shall see in a later chapter, in the early twentieth century, Ibn Rashid, ruler of Ha'il in northern Arabia, was vanquished by the British puppet Ibn Saud and his jihadis for identical reasons).

The annexation of the Awadh region occurred in 1856 but only after a media campaign against the existing nominal ruler accusing him of misrule, oppression and tyranny. The Governor-General of India, Dalhousie, had previously declared in 1855 that the Government of Awadh: "has been notorious for its abuse of power, for gross misrule, and for the oppression of its subjects."[40]

Indeed, one British newspaper article argued that the capital of Awadh was comparable to Gomorrah and was crying out for British annexation to redeem the condition of its people.[41] On 7 February 1856, Awadh was annexed and Dalhousie boasted that, "our gracious Queen [Victoria] has five million more subjects and £1,300,000 more revenue than she had yesterday."[42]

However, this particular annexation proved to be one too many. A year later, the soldiers (sepoys) and people of Awadh led the great revolutionary uprising of 1857 against the EIC which shook the British imperialist presence in India to its foundations.

The people of Awadh were joined by other regions in their liberation struggle against British imperialism as incarnated in EIC rule. Indian nationalists refer to the rebellion as India's first war of independence, while the imperialists continue to belittle it as a mere "mutiny" of soldiers who were presumably hitherto loyal to the British Queen. As historian Thomas Metcalf argues in his account on the aftermath of the war:

"There can be no doubt that sepoy discontent was an essential ingredient of the rebellion. Without it the popular outburst would never have taken place. But once the sepoys had risen, the Mutiny derived its real strength from the adherence of the civil population. The sepoy uprising was in fact little more than the spark which touched off a smouldering mass of combustible material."[43]

Two characteristics of the rebellion continue to confuse and cause pain to imperialists to this day. Firstly, the Empire felt many of the Indians who rebelled against them had "no legitimate reasons" to rebel as they in theory economically benefited from British rule.[44] Secondly, was the remarkable unity shown by Muslim and Hindu revolutionaries against the Empire.[45] On this basis, the deceptive notion of an "Indian Mutiny" was popularised to categorise the uprising. In effect, the notion of "Mutiny" helps to strictly localise the revolt to one particular demographic, i.e. sepoys or soldiers. Then on the basis of this categorisation it was easier to explain away or infantilise the cause of the rebellion as rooted in the EIC's lack of cultural sensitivity towards its soldiers when it compelled them to use rifle cartridges made with material considered to be holy to the sepoys.

The rebellion enveloped most of the northern Indian states, while some areas of India were immune to the rebellion. But even in those Indian states which are said to this day to have "held" or "remained loyal" (to use the historian Niall Ferguson's words)[46] to the EIC, they did so on the basis of pre-emptive measures taken by British imperialist soldiers as soon as the uprising began. For example, in the Punjab, as soon as news emerged that sepoys had rebelled, "all native regiments of dubious allegiance" were "disarmed, all forts and arsenals secured, and all treasure brought in from outlying districts and placed under guard."[47] Thousands of sepoys were quickly disengaged and disempowered by virtue of being "lined up before five companies of European troops and a battery of guns with port-fires lighted."[48] Anyone in the Punjab who verbally gave the slightest impression they sympathised with the liberation struggle was summarily executed because the British knew they were fighting an existential war for the Empire.[49]

When news reached Britain of the great revolutionary

upheaval taking hold of India, the nation united in its quest for vengeance and blood lust against what it perceived to be a lesser race.[50] Ferguson states that churches all over the country sermonised on the need for "revenge."[51] He quotes a Baptist preacher delivering a sermon to a mass congregation of 25,000 people in Crystal Palace, London, howling his blood-lust as such:

"The religion of the Hindoos is no more than a mass of the rankest filth that imagination ever conceived. The Gods they worship are not entitled to the least atom of respect. Their worship necessitates everything that is evil and morality must put it down. The sword must be taken out of its sheath, to cut off our fellow subjects by their thousands."[52]

Indeed, the very notion of a darker race rising up against white supremacy clearly caused a British identity crisis. As the historian Christopher Herbert writes, "[w]hat was unbearably horrible was not simply that British victims were cruelly sacrificed but that the sacrificers were black."[53]

The British nation was not disappointed with the Empire's response. The "fury of retribution that seized the nation" found ultimate expression in the Empire forcing captured resistance fighters and their sympathisers to wipe or lick blood from the pavement before their execution.[54] Stuffing Indians down cannons and blowing them out must have given a thrill to the imperialists and barbarically tickled many who were monitoring the antics of their heroes.[55] One writer who participated in the orgy of British vengeance notes that the "indiscriminate burning of villages, and the pillaging of 'niggers,' was the most costly amusement Europeans in India could indulge in."[56] One Indian historian, Amaresh Misra, claims that over a period of 10 years from 1857, the British killed 10 million Indians.[57]

After the revolt was crushed the Empire decided to rule solely through native puppet rulers and avoid directly annexing

Indian kingdoms altogether.[58] The reason it did this was because the Empire concluded, generally speaking, that the regions that had risen up in the liberation struggle against the EIC were those that were annexed and had their rulers deposed, while regions that were ruled via a Resident and his native puppet-ruler largely remained loyal to the EIC.[59] As Fisher argues, the "fighting of 1857 had as a prime cause the policy of annexation, which incited many Indian Rulers and former Rulers...to fight against the British."[60]

On the dead backs of tens of thousands of slaughtered Indians of different types of religious hew, it was scornfully realised and concluded that the most efficient way to bleed and plunder India was via a local lackey leader. Governor-General Canning, Dalhousie's successor, argued that ruling through a puppet was superior because they possess "a sympathy with and a hold over the feelings and hearts of the common herd [of Indians] which they cannot bequeath to us."[61]

In effect, the Empire concluded that one of the main ways to avoid further rebellions not only in India but anywhere in the Empire was to adopt the indirect rule system and rule through a native collaborator. The Empire found that this mode of occupation established "stability." That is, post 1858, the "British made the stability of the system of indirect rule a central pillar of the Empire."[62] Through this system of governance, it was hoped that resistance to the Empire would be minimalised because, in the words of Fisher, it "shielded Europeans from the potential hostility of the local population."[63] Furthermore, the EIC was operationally dissolved after the war and the British government took hold of calling the shots in India.

Ultimately, British rule in India was devastating and savage. Once again, before the Battle of Plassey, Dhaka in Bengal had exported 2.85 million rupees worth in textiles to Britain; by 1817 it was exporting no textiles at all.[64] An economic factor that contributed to this was that British goods produced by the new industrial revolution were protected by imposing high tariffs on Indian goods coming to Britain. Moreover, British goods exported to India were more competitive than indigenous produce because the EIC imposed higher tariffs on the latter.[65] Under British rule, India's "share of world manufacturing exports fell from 27% to 2%."[66]

Before the Battle of Plassey the population of Dhaka in Bengal was 150,000; by 1840 it had been reduced to 20,000. By the late-nineteenth century, famines had taken the lives of tens of millions of Indians. "Famines are wars," wrote Professor Mike Davis, "over the right to existence."[67] For the Empire, it was clear as day that some human existence was surplus to requirements. The Indian politician Shashi Tharoor claims that between 30 and 35 million Indians perished as a result of what he refers to as the "British Colonial Holocaust."[68] During an Indian famine in 1866 which took the lives of 1.5 million people, the Empire exported 200 million pounds of rice to Britain.[69] And India was not the only country impoverished by the Empire. For example, the indigenous Irish died in their millions as Britain looted Ireland's foodstuffs for England in the nineteenth century.

The Empire's material impoverishment of India was portrayed in the metropolis as the natural state of Indians and not the cruel outcome of the Empire's violence, conquest and economic policies. The British argued that the native's condition was borne out of his spiritual backwardness or indolence and this further justified the British presence in India as one of a civilising mission to uplift the native from his condition.[70]

To further consolidate its rule of India, the Empire promoted and then consolidated divisions between the two most populous religions in India, Muslims and Hindus. When there was no religions to pit against each other, they found sects of the same religion, (i.e. Sunnis and Shias) to disunify.[71]

During the period under Dr Fisher's study, there were 550 Indian states.[72] The "tentacles" of the Empire, as Malcolm X would say, would further stretch beyond India to neighbouring areas where the British Empire's interests needed to be made paramount. British-occupied territories in Africa correctly spring to mind when one seeks to find other examples of indirect rule.[73] However, one area that is overlooked is the Arab side of the Persian Gulf which was ruled by the Empire through a town in today's Iran, Bushire.

Persian Gulf

The Bushire base was established to safeguard the Empire's shipping into what is today Iraq. The influence of the Bushire 'Resident' covered the neighbouring Arab littoral, across the Gulf.[74] The Bushire Resident in turn was accountable to the Empire in India.

In 1853, the Empire formalised pre-existing treaties with the piratical sheikhs of Dubai, Abu Dubai, Ajman and others into a "Treaty of Peace in Perpetuity" with the aim of preventing attacks on EIC shipping.[75] It seems that at this point this posse of desert bandits became known as the "Trucial States."

In the 1860s Charles Aitchison, Foreign Secretary of the Indian Government, argued that the mainland of the Arabian Peninsula was not as important to the Empire as the security of the seas and it is on this basis that imperial agreements with these coastal bandits or "sheikhs" were made. As he argued: "Our true policy...is to make ourselves so strong at seas that we shall be respected, and if necessary feared and no pirate shall dare to lift his head, but to have as little connection with the quarrels and disturbances on shore as possible."[76]

In 1868, the British, through the Bushire Residency, installed its first Bahraini puppet, Ali bin Khalifah after the previous ruler, Muhammad bin Khalifah, had allegedly attacked British interests.[77] The latter escaped the clutches of the British to make a dramatic return a year later with his ally Muhammad bin Abdullah to depose and kill Ali. The Empire, seeing this scenario as a "challenge to British hegemony over the Gulf," decided to send in a squadron and established the killed sheikh's son, Issa bin Ali, as the ruler of Bahrain. Just over a decade later, the British Resident in Bushire "persuaded" Issa to: "refuse permission to any other government than the British to establish diplomatic or consular agencies or coaling depots in our territory, unless with the consent of the British Government."[78]

British imperialists have been living happily ever after with descendants of their Khalifah puppets. Recently, the British government founded a new military base, largely financed by the current Khalifah puppet, while the majority of the island are denied basic human rights or democracy.[79] As we have already seen, the notion of a puppet-ruler subsidising British imperialism for its own protection was a feature of British rule in India.[80]

Furthermore, with the opening of this British maritime military base in Bahrain in 2016, the London ambassador of this vassal state, Fawaz bin Muhammad al-Khalifa, boasted on the nature of contemporary British neo-colonialism. Bahrain, he claims "hosts...a large number of British companies: 500 British brands, 90 British company branches, and 350 Bahraini-British business partnerships. These businesses operate in some of Bahrain's key sectors, including banking, accounting, law and industry."[81] Bahrain is clearly another neo-colonial outlet for British business in all but name. But in all fairness to the puppet's representative, if they weren't "hosting" these businesses his family would be overthrown and the Empire would find another lackey.

The nineteenth-century history of Qatar is very much intertwined with that of Bahrain. It was then widely accepted that the ruler of Bahrain had suzerainty over the Qatar peninsula.[82] However, with the appearance of the Empire the situation began to change.

At the same time as it installed Isa bin Khalifah in Bahrain, the Political Resident of the Persian Gulf, Lewis Pelly, made a "Shaykh" – Muhammad bin Thani – the authority in some areas of Qatar. An agreement was signed in 1868 recognising Thani as a district ruler.[83] Pelly then warned the other Shaykhs and tribes of Qatar not to "molest him or his tribesman."[84] Herein began the first steps towards the independent entity we know today as Qatar. The Thani family rule Qatar to this day and it was the Empire that had originally installed them as rulers.

The al-Thani rule in Qatar was further consolidated when in the late-1870s they invaded and ransacked a town called Zubarah on the other side of the small Qatar peninsula, which the ruler of Bahrain had claimed.[85] This attack was clearly condoned by the Empire because when their puppet in Bahrain asked them to intervene on behalf of Zubarah's inhabitants, they refused.[86]

Qatar today is a state in its own right which ploughs billions of pounds into the British economy.[87] The tallest building in Europe, the Shard in London, was financed entirely by a Qatari sovereign fund owned by the Qatari state. The British media refer to Qatar as they do other Gulf countries' financial outlays in the United Kingdom as "investments" rather than "tributes" to their original imperial masters.

In 1892, the Empire further consolidated its rule over the aforementioned "Trucial States" by establishing outright paramountcy on who they were allowed to engage with. The new treaty prevented the rulers from entering into foreign relations with any other power, requiring the rulers to reject the establishment of any agent of a foreign power on their turf and not lease any part of their territory to a power other than the British Empire.[88] In 1971, the Trucial States were afforded independence by Britain and were renamed the United Arab Emirates. The leading families who signed the agreement in 1892 were more or less the same as the ones that are today ruling the desert kingdom.

At the turn of the twentieth century, a new fixation began to take over British imperialist strategic thinking, namely German expansionism. The Germans wanted to build a railway line from

Berlin to Baghdad with a hub in the Gulf in an area in what is today called Kuwait. The British paranoidly interpreted this scheme as a German move on Britain's hold on India. As such, a pirate called Mubarak al-Sabah killed his brother Muhammad al-Sabah as he slept to ascend to rulership in Kuwait in 1896. The Ottoman authorities, which nominally ruled this area, suspected that the British Resident in the Gulf "instigated the murder."[89] By 1899, the Empire had "obtained a secret bond from the Kuwaiti Shaikh similar to those obtained a decade earlier" with Bahrain and the Trucial sheikhs.[90]

Exiled in the domain of the Kuwaiti Shaikh during this period was the head of the Saudi clan, Abd al-Rahman al-Saud. When his son, Abd al-Aziz al-Saud, set out in 1902 to successfully capture Riyadh in the Najd region of the Arabian Peninsula in the midst of the night he did so with British weapons supplied to him by the Kuwaiti Shaikh.[91] Upon hearing that Riyadh had fallen to Ibn Saud, the Qatari ruler, al-Thani, converted to the Wahhabi sect.[92] Ibn Saud's later expansion across the Arabian Peninsula, as we see in a later chapter, was conducted in collusion and in accordance with British imperialist interests. To this day, Saudi Arabia and Qatar are the only Muslim countries whose state religion is wahhabism. Both states owe the origins of their existence today not to Allah but to British imperialism.

Current British influence in Oman can also be traced back to the late eighteenth century but it wasn't until the late-nineteenth century that the British established paramountcy over both the local ruler and also over French imperialist intrigue. In 1891, the British Empire in India secured "a declaration" from the ruler of Oman, Faisal, that "he would not lease or alienate any part of his territory to a foreign power without British consent." The historian Ravinder Kumar argues this all but "converted Oman into a protectorate."[93]

When in 1898 Faisal attempted to span his wings and offer the French a coaling station on his territory, British imperialist paranoia kicked in claiming that this proposal may eventually be converted into a "naval fortress." The Empire quickly convinced Faisal, by dint of gunships aimed at his domain, to ultimately cancel any naval offerings to the French and become once again a good character.[94] Soon after this episode, the British ruler of India, the Viceroy, Lord Curzon, appointed a new Political Agent to Musqat, a certain Major Percy J Cox who was later to be promoted to lead the Residency at Bushire.

By the first decade of the twentieth century, the British Foreign Secretary, Lansdowne, declared in the House of Commons that the Empire, "should regard the establishment of a naval base, or of a fortified base, in the Persian Gulf by any other Power as a grave menace to British interests, and we should certainly resist it with all the means at our disposal."[95]

The current status quo on the Arab side of the Persian Gulf clearly and absolutely has its roots in the Empire's Indian Residency system whereby the Empire calls the shots through a ruling collaborator. As late as 1955, the British Foreign Secretary, Harold Macmillan, was referring to the Sheikh of Abu Dhabi and the ruler of Oman as "our client Rulers."[96]

As can be seen, indirect rule proved to be financially fruitful to British capitalism after the discovery of oil in this region. It has allowed the British establishment to have priority over the wealth instead of the peoples of the wider Arab region or hinterland. When this indirect rule order, that is the British-installed puppets, were threatened by the call of Arab Nationalism and Communism in the immediate Cold War era, Britain helped to promote Islamism to fend off these ideological challenges.[97]

Macmillan's successor, Selwyn Lloyd, argued in the late 1950s that any change in the current Gulf should be "as far as possible in accordance with" British interests.[98] He stressed that: "any liberalisation of the regimes designed to meet genuine grievances or to mollify reformist elements shall not go so far as to cripple the powers of the Ruling Families or compel them to bow to nationalist demands at the expense of their own attachment to us."[99]

The formal "independence" of these British Raj created statelets in the 1970s allowed for the repackaging, disguising and recalibration of the British presence in the Persian Gulf. Much fanfare in the late 1960s was made about the British "retreat" from east of Suez but as an article in the American establishment's *Foreign Affairs* argued, this "last remnant of the British Raj"[100] will continue to host a British military presence: "It is proposed, however, that a British 'presence' shall continue in the Gulf through the use of existing airfields as staging posts for the Royal Air Force, as well as through occasional naval visits, specialised desert training for small British Army units, and most importantly, the provision of British officers and equipment for local armed forces."[101]

When Professor Stephen M. Walt of the *Israeli Lobby* fame claims that it was "easier to let local elites run" the Gulf rather than Britain or the United States taking over these statelets, he is absolutely correct and if the latter were to happen then this region may turn them "into sullen and resentful colonies."[102] This was the main conclusion reached by British imperialists after the 1857 revolution in India was crushed.

The recalibration of the British presence in the Gulf was motivated by the growing strength of revolutionary movements in the Persian Gulf and Oman. By reducing British imperialist visibility and misleadingly characterising it as a "retreat" it was hoped that the people in that region would no longer target British imperialism because an obvious British presence would "arouse hostility among the revolutionaries and the discontented, without providing the strength on the ground to combat that hostility."[103] Yet the rulers of these principalities would continue to go to Britain for "help and advice."[104]

In 2013, a BBC article by its Security Correspondent, Frank Gardener, quoted a report by a British establishment think tank, the Royal United Services Institute, which agreed with the aforementioned *Foreign Affairs* article that the so-called "retreat" wasn't what it was made out to be or, as the report claimed, "the formal withdrawal from major bases east of Suez did not signal the end of British military involvement there – far from it."[105]

The puppet Arab rulers of the Persian Gulf after the Iranian revolution were geo-politically repackaged as the Gulf Cooperation Council and more recently they are at times also referred to as "moderate Sunni States." As Bengal provided a springboard in the late eighteenth century for British imperialism to expand across the rest of India, states like Qatar and Saudi Arabia are providing Britain (and its Western allies) with a springboard to attack other Arab states who do not align to their foreign policy or commercial interests such as we have seen in Libya in 2011 and today's war on Syria.[106]

Chapter 4

How Imperial Decline Led to the Emergence of the "English-Speaking Peoples"

"As Britain knows, all predominant power seems for a time invincible, but, in fact, it is transient."
Tony Blair to the US Congress[1]

Ever since the end of World War Two, the United Kingdom and the United States are seen to have sung from the same hymn sheet in war, peace and trade. Their alliance is perceived to be an amicable, natural and trans-historical partnership between two nations who share the same language and whose global interests are more or less the same. So it is no surprise that many find it hard to accept that this alliance is a relatively recent advent rooted in geo-political exigencies of the historical moment at hand. In this chapter, an overview of how British imperialism traversed from a foe of the American Republic in the nineteenth century to an ally in the twentieth century is provided.

Writing, if not gloating, in the midst of the American civil war in the nineteenth century, the future British Prime Minister Lord Salisbury (aka Robert Cecil) heralded not only the end of the United States of America but democracy itself or, as he referred to it, the "evil of universal suffrage."[2] American democracy and the vaunted Republic he gleefully boasted were not only a failed experiment and a busted flush but the "most ignominious failure the world had ever seen." It had become, in our esteemed Lord's eyes, what today would be referred to derogatively and pejoratively as a "failed state."

The main reason for this inevitable failure according to Cecil was that the United States had rejected and overthrown its natural leaders, i.e. the British establishment. As such they were now richly "reaping a harvest that was sown as far back as the time of Jefferson." The Americans had substituted genuine leadership for a dreamer's theory (the works of Thomas Jefferson) and more so, in the present climate, Abraham Lincoln was an "ass," an incompetent and "the most conspicuous cause of the present calamities."[3]

Another British Prime Minister, William Gladstone, also had little time for Lincoln and came out in support of the Southern Confederacy. The Gladstone family had become wealthy largely owing to the family's slave camps in Jamaica and William's maiden speech in Parliament was a defence of the family business which arose from the slave trading port of Liverpool. Although William Gladstone represented constituents in the family's native Parliamentary seat of Midlothian, Scotland, his father had represented Liverpool in Parliament.[4]

At the time of the civil war, Liverpool's economy as well as that of the wider north-west region of England was mostly reliant on cotton imported from the American south and then distributed to the cotton mills of Lancashire and Cheshire. Lincoln's Union army's blockade of Southern ports caused a massive disruption to this trade.

The blockade also affected the South's ship manufacturing facilities. As such, they turned to Great Britain for ship and gunboat manufacturing. Two ships stand out. The first was the *Alabama* which sunk 65 Union ships. The other Confederate ship was a trade ship re-fitted as a gunboat, *Shenandoah*, which once sent out to battle "captured nearly 40 prizes," i.e. that is hijacked and looted 40 Union and other ships. Needless to say the crew on both ships were mostly manned by British personnel.[5] Claims were made that these ships were "decoying their victims with the British flag."[6]

In Parliament, 74 members were in favour of the Confederacy, while only 17 were pro North, that is, pro Lincoln.[7] The British political establishment was clearly waiting for the right time to intervene on behalf of the South yet at the same time they were loathe to spread the Empire's resources "too thinly across the globe."[8]

In September 1862, the Empire felt the time had arisen to recognise the Confederacy. The two factors which determined this judgement were the Confederacy's defeat of the northern army of the Potomac in Manassas and its subsequent invasion of Maryland. After the two armies fought to a standstill in Maryland, the Confederacy troops retreated back to their stronghold, Virginia. On the back of this battle, Lincoln issued the "Emancipation Declaration" which the British Prime Minister, Lord Palmerston, condemned as illegal, hypocritical and against the American constitution.[9] The British establishment was joined by many British workers who too greeted the Proclamation with cynical disdain and they doubled down with support for the South.[10] *The Guardian* newspaper claimed that the "people are not so easily deluded" by the Proclamation, and continued to support the South and charmingly referred to Lincoln as a despot:[11] a now common pejorative deployed against any leader not considered conducive to the British establishment's interests.

However, all was not lost for the Empire and Palmerston earmarked May or June 1863 as the best time to recognise the pro-slavery South. But in the 1860s armour plated vessels began to be introduced to navy fleets. The French had introduced theirs in 1859, while the British introduced *HMS Warrior* in 1860. The Confederacy's *Virginia* was introduced in 1862; the Union unleashed the *USS Monitor* very shortly after.

Watching the battle from the sidelines, it dawned on the Empire that the Union ship was more technologically advanced than their *Warrior* and moreover many more were under construction in northern ports. The British carried out tests to see if the Empire's navy could withstand the new Union firepower. They couldn't and it was reasoned that if the Empire now intervened on behalf of the South, it would be only a matter of time before the North sent its ships across the Atlantic and rendered Her Majesty's "wooden fleet in great peril."[12] The Empire did not intervene in the American civil war because the establishment theorised that the Union could potentially retaliate and defend itself.

In 1863 the good people of Manchester burned an effigy of Lincoln on Guy Fawkes Night and, of course, when the war was over the highly esteemed good people of Manchester built a statue in his honour[13] or as one historian wrote, a dead Lincoln "was no danger; nothing could be lost and peace of mind could then be gained by lauding his neglected virtues."[14] The Empire also paid compensation to the United States for lost ships at the hands of the British.

It was not then until the late Victorian period that the United States and United Kingdom once again came close to crossing swords. A dispute arose between the British Empire's colony British Guiana and the independent state of Venezuela. The latter since more or less its creation earlier in the nineteenth century had made persistent claims to territory in British Guiana. The Empire on the other hand had the power to contemptuously brush these claims aside.

The Empire's delineation of the boundary between Venezuela and Guiana was based on the results of a survey conducted by Robert Schomburgk, the envoy of British Prime Minister Lord Palmerston, in 1835. This boundary came to be known as the Schomburgk Line. Venezuela had claimed that this boundary line was wrong and furthermore once gold mines were discovered the Empire extended its reach and claimed more of Venezuelan territory.

After many years of appealing to the Empire to no avail the Venezuelans were left no choice but to enlist the support of the United States. Richard Olney, a Secretary of State under President Grover Cleveland's administration, sent a strongly worded note to the Empire on 20 July 1895. Olney, in the note, invoked the

Monroe Doctrine, which meant no European nation (and that included Britain) had a right to newly intervene or impose itself in the Western hemisphere. For the then British Prime Minister Lord Salisbury (aka Robert Cecil), like many of the elite of his generation, the United States "counted for little in international affairs."[15] As such, he did not immediately respond and did not even warrant Olney's note a response until 26 November 1895. Salisbury rejected American claims to arbitration and furthermore argued that the Monroe Doctrine did not apply to the dispute between the Empire and Venezuela. For Salisbury the Monroe Doctrine had no universal legislative authority.

Upon this response, President Cleveland successfully asked the United States Congress to authorise a boundary commission whose findings would be enforced "by every means."[16] The Empire at this time was entangled in disputes elsewhere and was also keeping a keen eye on the rise of new powers in Europe (i.e. Germany) and the Far East (i.e. Japan). Therefore, it was not in a position to potentially stretch itself into another conflict. Furthermore, Great Britain's land grab for gold mines in southern Africa known as the "Jameson Raid" had failed. Knowing that war with the United States at this moment may strengthen its immediate adversaries in Europe, the Empire eventually acquiesced to American requests. Initially the Empire wanted to limit the geographical territory to be placed under arbitration. The Americans refused and the Empire capitulated and accepted unlimited arbitration.

The United States' threat of war combined with the potential of imperialist overreach brought the Empire to the negotiating table over the boundary dispute. How ironic that Robert Cecil more or less 30 years after mocking and denigrating the United States during its civil war became the first British Prime Minister to capitulate and appease the Republic.

In 1898, the military confrontation between the United States and the Spanish Empire arose. Although a myth has been circulated that the British were "tacitly" on the side of the Americans nothing could be further from the truth.[17] Five days before the American congress insisted on Spain getting out of Cuba, the British ambassador in Washington congregated other European ambassadors and was partly responsible for drafting a proposal critical of the United States position "which was referred to their governments for approval."[18] After Spain made concessions to the United States with regard to Cuba, the British ambassador and his European counterparts met once again to avert war. This time they recommended that their respective governments make representation to the United States' embassies in six European capitals.[19] Britain did not do anything to assist its European partner largely because its focus was on defending its imperial interests in Asia and Africa, rather than defending Imperial Spain. This was not pro-Americanism simply national and imperial self-interest.[20]

In October 1899, as the British century was coming to an end, the second Boer War ignited between the Empire and the two South African European colonies of the Orange Free State and Transvaal. The Empire captured the Transvaal capital in June 1900. Between September and October 1900 a general election was called which returned Lord Salisbury to power. However, in South Africa, guerrilla warfare took hold of the country. The Empire's forces under the leadership of Lord Roberts and Lord Kitchener finally crushed the resistance with a scorched earth policy, holding women and children in concentration camps and covering the country with barbed wire and blockhouses.[21] The Boers finally surrendered in May 1902.

In the late Victorian era the Empire's intellectuals were also wrestling with their consciousnesses over the ever-increasing competitiveness of the global order. The main factor that fuelled this apprehensive state of geo-political consciousness was the rise of Germany, the United States and Russia. The economies of Germany and the United States were seen as threats because they were more than just challenging British industrial supremacy. In 1870 the United Kingdom had more than the upper hand when it came to "world manufacturing production" with 31.8 per cent against 23.3 per cent for the United States and 13 per cent for Germany. By the end of 1885, it was 26.6 per cent, 28.6 per cent and 13.9 per cent respectively and at the start of the new century (1900) the United States had clearly surpassed the UK, 30.1 per cent to 19.5 per cent respectively with Germany on the heels of the latter with 16.6 per cent.[22] The trajectory was brutally clear: Great Britain was in relative economic decline.[23] While Tsarist Russia on the other hand was seen not so much as a direct economic threat to the Empire but as a nation with impossible intentions towards "British India." The Indian uprising of 1857 and its subsequent repression disinvested the Empire of any notion that its rule there was attuned to the willing consent, as hitherto believed, of the indigenous population.[24] The British pillage and impoverishment of India also had reached its zenith in the late Victorian era. The main periods of this impoverishment were the famines of 1876-9, 1889-91 and 1896-1902. Russia, it was feared, might tap into Indian resentment towards the Empire, agitate the masses and with their help dislodge British imperialism from its prized possession.

The challenges posed by this triad of Germany, the United States and Tsarist Russia, according Professor Duncan Bell in his study of "Greater Britain," "led to a reappraisal of Britain's global role and spurred the development of a mosaic of schemes for colonial unity."[25] Initially intellectuals perceived and wished to bring forth a "Greater Britain" as a "bulwark" against the new rising powers. This construct would be a new federal state consisting of the United Kingdom and its white settler colonies in North America (i.e. Canada), Oceania (Australia and New Zealand) and the colonies in southern Africa. Together they would be united in a federal parliament and hold their own in an ever more economically and militarily competitive world.

However, even this theoretical project failed to alleviate the gloom of what they perceived to be the coming dark clouds of time. The formula of Time for Empire they rightly reasoned determined that they rise and fall and the "ancients seemed to teach little" with regard to imperial preservation. Yet these intellectuals knew the "empire had to escape the clutches of time..." or more accurately imperial time, circular time which has been the destiny of all previous empires.[26] That is, all empires rise and fall.

Although British intellectuals identified their Empire with ancient Rome they didn't want it to end in ruin like Rome.[27] As with Rome in its pomp, the British Empire for the moment was militarily incomparable and as such had no need of allies. This incomparability allowed the Empire to have an "isolationist" foreign policy. This isolationism is not to be mistaken with the legend of American isolationism which is rooted in their "founding fathers" theoretic instruction not to become entangled in foreign affairs. British isolationism (or "splendid isolation" as historians grandiosely refer to it) in the latter part of the Victorian era is not rooted in any principled or idealistic notion of abstaining from foreign adventurism but in the fact that the Empire during peace time had no need of allies. No other nation, power or imperialist pretender could directly threaten the essence of the British Empire. Britannia was a modern Rome. It ruled the waves. However, from studying other previous empires, they knew this superiority wasn't to be indefinite. The writing was not so much on the wall, but in the history books. Relative economic decline further fuelled this foreboding. As the historian Niall Ferguson wrote in his bestseller *Empire: How Britain Made the Modern World*, the British "knew too much ancient history to be complacent about their hegemonic power... there were many who looked forward uneasily to the decline and fall of their own empire, like all the empires before it."[28]

At this point, a point determined by the "uneasiness" of

economics, the rise of imperial competitors and the trajectory of imperial history, the Empire reappraised its geo-political relationships with other nations. And it was within this context that previous attitudes towards the United States were abandoned. Up until well into the second half of the nineteenth century, the US "was regarded with a mixture of unease and disdain."[29] The reason for this is because the United States had more democratic rights for its (white) citizens and it defined itself as apart from the British Empire and the rest of Europe. The military and political concept and alliance we today understand as an American-led "West" did not gain traction until after World War Two when a face-off with the Soviet Union "East" became more pronounced.

Furthermore, as the past gave no reassurances that a "Greater Britain" would be enough for the continuation of the Empire, some intellectuals:

"sought authority in the image of America. This move was the result of the perceived consequences of understanding empires as transient, temporary, and above all, self-dissolving. In order to defend a permanent global Anglo-Saxon polity, they tried to escape this trajectory, to anchor their vision in secure temporal foundations. Greater Britain was to be located in a progressive narrative, open to the future not condemned by the past."[30]

British intellectuals were determined to wrench their Empire from history's inevitable damnation and avoid the flames that await all imperial hubris. In the interests of self-preservation, comparisons with past empires were cast aside in exchange for "secure temporal foundations." Specifically they re-orientated "their gaze toward America, shifting the source of inspiration from the past to the present – all in the name of the future. America was to be a substitute...an apposite political structure,...

an imaginative means to escape the dangers heralded by the past."[31] Indeed, the United States was no longer to be regarded as "a potential or actual competitor but rather as a partner in the quest for global progress."[32]

A common linguistic expression was appropriated to encapsulate this potential rapprochement and future entente. The term "English-Speaking Peoples" may today seem innocuous but its contemporary usage is firmly rooted in the limitations of the notion of "Greater Britain" to fend off imperial decline and the wish to incorporate its former colony (and the new rising world power) the United States, into its world view. The essayist Christopher Hitchens was mistaken when he claimed the expression "English-speaking" is merely a "synonym for 'English' by blood.'"[33] At the very least, the expression was conceived, according to a British historian, "as a common endeavour in which the historic breach between the United States and the British Empire was to be healed."[34]

In 1900, the Prime Minister, Lord Salisbury, relinquished the foreign ministry portfolio he had attached to his premiership and appointed the Marquess of Lansdowne as the Empire's new Foreign Secretary. Quickly Lansdowne initiated what came to be referred to as a "new course" in foreign policy which can be seen as encapsulating the zeitgeist of apprehensive imperial thinking of the preceding years. Europe had formed into military alliances and blocs which the Empire could no longer ignore. On the one hand, there was the France-Russia alliance which was cemented in a treaty in 1892, on the other was the Triple alliance of Germany, Italy and Austria-Hungary.

Russia continued to be perceived as a menace and potential threat to Great Britain's hold on India. It was feared that Russia might take advantage of the Empire's travails in its cumbersome crushing of the Boers and agitate in India. It didn't but the United States seemed to notice the Empire's position. The Empire, in the late 1890s, had many disputes between the United States and

Canada over trade rights in fishing and fur seal fishing. But the two major disputes were the border between Alaska and Canada and the proposed Isthmian Canal connecting the Atlantic and Pacific oceans.

American citizens had settled in parts of Alaska which Canada had made claims to especially after gold mines had been discovered in specific regions. The United States also wanted to revisit the 1850 Clayton-Bulwer Treaty that was signed with Great Britain in the event of a canal being built across the Isthmian linking the two great oceans. The treaty guaranteed inter alia the canal's military neutrality. Initially Lord Salisbury wanted to link the two issues and only concede to the Americans on total claims to the canal in exchange for American concessions on the Alaska-Canada border.[35] The Americans refused and insisted on addressing both issues on their individual merits.

Furthermore, with the rise of new imperial powers – European military alliances on its doorstep and most importantly the Empire's forces bogged down in South Africa – the British had no choice but to cave in and appease the Americans. "The war stretched British resources to their limit at a time when public feeling on the Continent was pressing the great Powers to intervene in the struggle to save the Boers"[36] wrote the historian J. Grenville, and a new treaty, known as the Hay-Pauncefote Treaty, was eventually signed in November 1901. This agreement guaranteed the United States ownership and military supremacy in the future development of the canal across the Isthmian. The agreement surrendered military supremacy to the United States in the western hemisphere not out of choice, ideology or kinship but out of imperial necessity.[37]

Nevertheless the Empire continued to fantasise about invading the United States. A pre-emptive war plan to invade the United States on three fronts: a land invasion from Montreal coupled with landings on New York and Boston was drawn up. The invasion was to be supported by a prospective uprising of

Native Americans who would no doubt come running to the assistance of the British.[38] Unfortunately the Empire was never in a military position to materialise this adventure.

The capitulation to the United States was one of the first agreements made by Lansdowne that allowed him to consolidate the Empire's resources to where its main interests lay, namely in Africa and Asia. Up until 1901 British naval policy was, in theory, based on parity with the two next major naval powers.[39] This policy was no longer sustainable. The rise of new powers and alliances being formed among its imperial competitors rendered it redundant and the Empire sought to establish its own alliances. British eyes were on the France-Russian Alliance which had held since 1894. It was feared their combined strength posed not only a threat to the Empire's global possessions but also to the home waters. Therefore, the British fleet needed first and foremost to account for the metropolis and in such a case this "made it impossible to maintain British supremacy in the Caribbean and Pacific as well."[40]

Within 3 months of signing away military supremacy to the United States in the western hemisphere, Great Britain entered an agreement with Japan in the Far East. In this agreement the Empire pledged to support Japan in any war with an adversary if a third party became involved. In practice this meant that if Japan and Russia decided to go to war and France came to the assistance of Russia, the British Empire would be obliged to join on the side of Japan. Japan saw this agreement as a green light to expand while the British saw it as a way of checking Tsarist Russia expansionism in Asia and obviously and specifically India.

Amid the war between Russia and Japan in 1904-5, the Empire signed the "Entente Cordial" with the French. Both nations were apprehensive about the rise of Germany and entered this alliance as a bulwark against any German expansionism. The Empire made another alliance with Tsarist Russia later in the decade.

The alliances made and initiated by Lansdowne in his term as Foreign Secretary held for another 10 years and were carried into the Great War or World War One intact. That is, the tripartite of the British Empire, France and the Tsar's Russia were pitted against a German-led alliance which included the Ottoman Empire in an imperialist carnage to carve up mankind for their own benefit.

Although the British had the support of its Empire spanning a quarter of the world, even this was not enough to defeat Germany. A media campaign to entice its former colony, the United States, to assist it in the war began.

The British were in a good position to entice the Americans to win the war for them for four main reasons. Firstly, because Americans saw Europe "through a distinctly British perspective. Few American newspapers at that time maintained European staffs of their own; while those that which did found few trained American trained foreign correspondents to man them."[41] Secondly, the British cut off the communication channels between Germany and America therefore all news to the United States was further filtered through the British censor.[42] Thirdly, the British in their propaganda in the United States made out that the interests of the British Empire were also American interests. Some newspapers thought that the Empire was fighting America's battle and the future of democracy was at stake although Britain's ally was the autocratic Russia of the Tsar and the British had never instituted democracy among the indigenous populations of Africa and Asia it lorded over. The propaganda worked to the extent that "the British captured the American flag and waved it in front of themselves."[43] Fourthly, and most importantly, the British economically tied good proportions of the American economy and business into the war with purchases of arms ware and loans and therefore "made American business dependent upon a British victory."[44] The Empire was eventually "saved from collapse" in the Great

War by the United States' entry in April 1917.[45]

The British imperialist establishment felt no shame or disgrace in endearing itself to a nation it had tried to strangle on more than one occasion. The Empire had attempted to crush the American revolution, it then invaded the United States in 1814 and burned the capital, Washington, to the ground and during the civil war the British did all they could to see a partition of the United States by supporting the Confederacy in all but name. In all three cases the British Empire failed in their objective of destroying the United States. With Britain's imminent economic and military decline foreseen, the British establishment in the late Victorian era shamelessly began to promote potential refuge and security under an American wing. During World War One, the Empire with most of the world's resources and people at hand had no choice but to rope in the United States to its war with Germany.

History repeated itself in World War Two. The British Empire found itself up against the Germans again and as Winston Churchill said during his short spell at the Admiralty in 1940, it was one thing delighting the British populace with slaughtering less technologically developed Africans and Asians ("harmless objects") and another fighting Germans:

"Indeed one may look back with envy to the past, and to the Victorian Age when great controversies were fought about what now seem to us very minor matters. When great states fought little wars and when the pugnacious instincts of our people were satisfied with such comparatively harmless objects as Cetewayo, the Mahdi, President Kruger and the Mad Mullah – I mean the Mad Mullah of Somaliland."[46]

The "Empire alone could not have won the Second World War"[47] wrote Ferguson and as late as 1927 Churchill had even contemplated the Empire waging war on the United States[48] but when the Japanese attacked Pearl Harbour in 1941, Britain's greatest ever hero literally danced and jigged. He knew that American entry into the war would guarantee his and British imperialist survival. The Empire was saved from behind an American command, like the playground bully who when a more revolting bully arrives on the scene scurries behind a stronger saviour. Thereafter, the United States declared war on Japan and only after Germany and Italy declared war on the United States in solidarity with their Japanese ally did the Americans several days later declare war on the fascists of Europe.

There is nothing naturally inevitable about the current alliance between the United Kingdom and the United States of America. It was disingenuous of Christopher Hitchens to argue that the origins of the current geo-political relationship between the United States and the British state is to be "sought in the grand triad of race, class, and empire – the trivium upon which the relationship rests,"[49] when in fact it is to be actually, empirically and corroboratively found in British imperialism's global economic and military decline.

If India in 1857 had successfully emulated the United States and thrown off the shackles of British imperialism, the British Empire's decline would have clearly happened much sooner as there would not have been a guaranteed market for its goods, foodstuffs to plunder for its own people or an Indian auxiliary army to defend the Empire and subjugate other nations. Although the Empire could throttle and crush the Indian nation and other parts of the world in the latter part of the nineteenth century and early twentieth century, it could not prevent the challenge and rise of the United States, Germany and other European powers. It is within this decline of imperial power coupled with the rise of other nations that today's alliance of the United Kingdom with the United States originates. The fanciful and appropriated expression "English-Speaking Peoples" (or in the age of Brexit, the "Anglosphere") is a linguistic masquerade of this imperial decline and an "implicit" acknowledgement that British imperialism and with it the British establishment would not survive without the power of the United States.[50]

Chapter 5

British Imperialism Takes Grip of the Middle East

This chapter is divided into three sections and because they deal with the same period and the same region, the area that came to be known as the "Middle East," some of the sections will inevitably overlap. Each of the sections provides an overview on how the British Empire established itself in today's Arab World.

In the beginning, Britain fully established itself in the Arab World during World War One and there is no more iconic figure in this episode than so-called "Lawrence of Arabia" who led the so-called Arab revolt against the Ottoman Empire. So the first section delves into why the British had no choice but to support an "Arab Revolt." T. E. Lawrence's much vaunted *Seven Pillars of Wisdom* is the main source to uncover the truth of what lay behind the revolt.

The second section deals with why the British wanted to establish a Zionist colony in Palestine and how they denied democracy to the indigenous population. This denial led to the Palestinian ethnic cleansing by British-trained Zionist settlers.

The third section looks at how the Kingdom of Saudi Arabia was established by the British Empire because they needed a ruler in Mecca and Madina, the two holiest places of Islam, who would not be averse to Britain's Zionist project in Palestine.

Section 1: T. E. Lawrence: The World War One Defeats That Made an Imperialist Swindler

"By our swindle they were glorified...The more we condemned and despised ourselves, the more we could cynically take pride in them, our creatures...They were our dupes, wholeheartedly fighting the enemy."
T. E. Lawrence, Seven Pillars of Wisdom[1]

The enemy Thomas Edward Lawrence (aka "Lawrence of Arabia") is referring to in the above quote is none other than the Turkish Ottoman Empire. The people who were "swindled" and "duped" were the Arabs who were convinced and manipulated to take up arms and rise up in an "Arab Revolt" a hundred years ago, against their Turkish overlords in support of the British Empire's war effort during World War One.

The Ottoman Empire entered the war on the side of Germany in November 1914. In the United Kingdom, many thought the war would end quickly and everyone would be home for Christmas because the British populace were weaned on stories of imperialist heroics administering the natives of Asia and Africa a military beating in a surprisingly short amount of time. As the writer and academic Adam Hochschild wrote on the centenary of the war: "Colonial wars seldom lasted long because the German, French and British Armies had modern rifles, machine guns and small mobile artillery pieces, as well as steamboats and railroads that could move men and weapons as needed. The Africans and Asians usually had none of these things."[2]

Unsurprisingly, millions in Britain immediately enrolled to fight Germany only to find that they too were shockingly fighting with the latest military technology. To overcome the stalemate that quickly transpired on the western front, i.e. the war in

Europe, the British came up with a supremely cunning idea of prioritising the defeat of Germany's ally, the Ottoman Empire, in the hope of hastening a quick and decisive victory.[3] On this basis, the primary and most important military strategy was an attack through the Strait of Dardanelles to capture Istanbul, the seat and capital of the Ottoman Empire.

Winston Churchill, First Lord of the Admiralty, advocated the idea of a naval expedition to sail through the Strait of Dardanelles and capture Istanbul at a British war cabinet meeting on 13 January 1915.[4] However, an argument has been made that the idea, in the event of war, can be traced back to 1906.[5] Lord Kitchener, Secretary of State for War (a cabinet position which was precursor to today's Defence Secretary) thought that the Turks would automatically flee at the first sight of His Majesty's naval forces entering and sailing up the straits without the British requiring to land or fight elsewhere: "Kitchener felt that the Ottoman garrison on the Gallipoli Peninsula would flee and surrender without requiring the landing of British troops."[6]

This military assumption was understandable as Kitchener had gained his reputation by scoring courageous military victories against indigenous populations in Africa and Asia who had limited (if any) technological hardware to defend themselves. This was also why there was such a popular clamouring for his appointment to the British war government at the outbreak of war from his previously held position as the Proconsul of Egypt.

Arrogantly, British imperialism had not anticipated the Ottomans would put up a defence largely because they had convinced themselves the Turks were a lesser breed to themselves, a "master race" with an Empire upon which the sun did not cast its shadow. More so, the Ottoman Empire was constantly referred to before the war as the "sick man of Europe" and, as we know, sick people are too weak to put up a defence. Accordingly, it was with "some relish" that the British Prime Minister, Herbert H. Asquith, "contemplated the prospect of war against Turkey."[7] "Few things" he stated "would give me greater pleasure than to see the Turkish Empire finally disappear from Europe."[8]

The British Empire's Royal Navy attack on the straits began in February 1915 and was quickly considered a failure in March 1915. Therein, the campaign morphed from a solely navy exercise into an amphibious expedition.[9] As *The Times* was to explain during the centenary commemoration in 2015, "The land assault was launched after the failure of a campaign to force the Dardanelles by sea power alone."[10]

The new re-organised campaign in the Dardanelles was an enterprise led by the British Empire with contributions from Irish, Australians, New Zealand and Indian battalions as well as French.

On 25 April 1915, the British Empire led forces landed on Cape Helles, while Australian and New Zealand troops landed at "Anzac Cove" on the Gallipoli Peninsula. Both landings were fended off by Ottoman forces. Other attempts by the British Empire were easily repelled by the Ottomans in May and June,[11] forcing Churchill to resign in May 1915. Throughout the summer, small scale clashes continued but a new offensive was launched by the British Empire in August 1915 to capture Istanbul. The new campaign was headed by General Sir Federick Stopford, an extremely great Britisher of strong repute who like Kitchener had earned his reputation during the Boer War against a rag-tag militia army. This attack was launched on 6 August, successfully repelled on 10 August and the good "General Sir" was delivered an imperial royal boot and sacked on 15 August. Over the next 4 months the fighting "petered out" as one historian put it.[12] However, the truth is that the British government couldn't face informing its own population that the British Empire had been defeated in southern Europe by non-Europeans. British imperialist bureaucrats in London, Delhi and Cairo "all feared for the consequences of British rule were they seen to have been defeated by an 'Asiatic' enemy."[13] In other words, the much maligned "wogs" had defeated the privately educated led British Empire and the latter didn't know how to square this with their minions back in the metropolis.

As the complete failure of the Dardanelles campaign dawned on British imperialism, British Foreign Secretary Sir Edward Grey informed the war cabinet that they were "practically bankrupt of prestige in the East." The decision to finally throw in the towel at Gallipoli was made on 22 November 1915.

Two other military defeats in 1915 also need to be noted to fully appreciate T. E. Lawrence's "swindle."

Firstly, just before the Dardanelles campaign was launched, British imperialism encouraged its protégé, the so-called Emir of Najd (an area in the centre of the Arabia Peninsula), Abd al-Aziz Ibn Saud, and his fanatical Wahhabi-jihadi henchmen to attack the Ottoman Empire's ally, Ibn Rashid, in the north of the Arabian Peninsula.

Grey despatched a certain William Shakespear as "Political Officer on Special Duty" on 9 October 1914, to re-establish communication with the Emir of Najd, with a view that in the "event of war with Turkey, to make certain of Arab goodwill."[14] Shakespear set out to join Ibn Saud on 12 December 1914 and arrived, via Kuwait, at his side on 31 December 1914.

Several days later, Shakespear wrote to Gertrude Bell (the Orientalist and the architect of the Middle East's first ever 96 per cent election victory) that Ibn Saud "is making preparations for a big raid on Ibn Rashid with a view to wiping him out practically and I shouldn't be surprised if I reached Hail in the course of the next month as Bin Saud's political adviser."[15]

Ibn Rashid was a Turkish ally from Hail, a town in northern Arabia. Unfortunately, it was Shakespear that was "wiped out" with a bullet in his head when battle occurred on 24 January 1915. Ibn Saud's wahhabi fanatics were defeated but Shakespear's legacy lives as the first ever British martyr of wahhabism.

It wasn't until almost 2 months later that the British establishment officially acknowledged Shakespear's death. In an editorial, *The Times* noted that Shakespear "is believed to have succumbed to wounds received" in the battle, alongside the "Anglophile Ibn Saud."[16] Anglophile here clearly means being a British-backed puppet and not a man of letters as Ibn Saud was simply not noted for having any interest in literature, Arabic or English.

However, the British Political Agent in Kuwait, Colonel William Grey, attempted to depoliticise Shakespear's death claiming that it was caused by a "stray bullet in a small tribal skirmish."[17] And it is this lie that Lawrence poetically regurgitates in his monumental *Seven Pillars of Wisdom* when he claims Shakespear was "killed in battle by the Shammar in a set-back which the champions of Nejd had suffered during one of their periodic wars."[18] In effect, Lawrence cleverly re-contextualises Shakespear's death from one rooted in World War One to a tribal war.

This defeat almost brought an end to Ibn Saud's rule in Najd and certainly knocked "him out of action for a year."[19] But his military stock was quickly replenished by the British to the extent that he was able to quash local uprisings of tribes that had never accepted the British puppet. Therefore, when the Middle East expert Professor Eugene Rogan of Oxford University states that "Ibn Saud had no interest in fighting the Ottomans in Arabia," he is far from being correct. [20]

Secondly, the main intention behind Shakespear's failed mission was to complement the British Empire's campaign in the Persian Gulf.[21] The Empire successfully invaded and captured Basra, in what is now southern Iraq, on 21 November 1914. By the summer of 1915 the entire province of Basra had been captured. However, the British wanted a "glittering success" to offset the inevitable announcement of defeat at Gallipoli or rather undo any "perceived damage to imperial prestige."[22] It was then decided to occupy Baghdad. According to the British Empire's Viceroy in Delhi: "the capture of Baghdad would create an immense impression in the Middle East, especially in Persia, Afghanistan, and on our frontier, and would counteract the unfortunate impression created by the want of success in the Dardanelles."[23]

The British advance to Baghdad was halted at Ctesphion in November 1915, 30 kilometres south-west of the city. Thereupon they retreated to Kut al-Amara which they had captured in September 1915. There they were besieged by the Ottoman forces or as Lawrence writes, "abruptly checked. We fell back, dazed; and the long misery of Kut began."[24] The British Empire did attempt to reinforce its army by sending two infantry divisions from France and one from the Dardanelles to relieve the situation but it was all to no avail as the forces of the British Empire succumbed to the siege and surrendered on 29 April 1916.

This left the British imperialists with no other option but to rely upon a correspondence with the Sharif of Mecca in the Hijaz, the western part of the Arabian Peninsula. The new correspondence between the British agent in Egypt, Henry McMahon, and the Sharif of Mecca, Hussain bin Ali, began in July 1915 and came to an end in January 1916.

The idea of utilising Arab aspirations for independence from the Ottoman Empire to the advantage of the British Empire can be traced back to early 1914 and Lawrence credits Kitchener as the main driver behind this strategy: "Some Englishmen of whom Kitchener was chief, believed that a rebellion of Arabs against Turkey would enable England while fighting Germany, simultaneously to defeat her ally Turkey."[25]

The Sharif naively read McMahon's correspondence as assurances of a commitment by the British to keep their word and grant Arabs a united independent country stretching from Gaza, covering all of Syria (what today is also divided into

Palestine/Israel, Jordan, Lebanon), Baghdad and the Arabian Peninsula once the war was over. But Lawrence knew the correspondence should be seen in wider context. As he wrote: "Our check in Mesopotamia was a disappointment to us; but McMahon continued his negotiations with Mecca, and finally brought them to success despite evacuation of Gallipoli, the surrender of Kut, and the generally unfortunate aspect of the war at the moment."[26]

Ironically on the very day the Arab Revolt began, 5 June 1916, the Germans blasted Lord Kitchener to Kingdom Come while on *HMS Hampshire* in the North Sea. This imperialist white supremacist was certainly not the "red-coated imperial hero" as Christopher Hitchens glowingly lauded him.[27] A life time of imperialist heroics against the natives of Africa and Asia had come to a drenched end at the bottom of the sea at the hands of an enemy equally adept with modern technology. Kitchener's death brought home a truism to the British establishment, already mentioned in the previous chapter of this book (which needs repeating), that it was one thing to invade, occupy and slaughter the darker shades of humanity but quite another to wage war on Germany as Churchill conceded in the first months of World War Two:

"Indeed one may look back with envy to the past, and to the Victorian Age when great controversies were fought about what now seem to us very minor matters. When great states fought little wars and when the pugnacious instincts of our people were satisfied with such comparatively harmless objects as Cetewayo, the Mahdi, President Kruger and the Mad Mullah – I mean the Mad Mullah of Somaliland."[28]

Returning to Lawrence, who knew the promises, assurances and commitments made by McMahon were lies and not worth the paper they were written on: "It was evident from the beginning that if we won the war these promises would be dead paper, and had I been an honest advisor of the Arabs I would have advised them to go home and not risk their lives fighting for such stuff…" because as he acknowledged, what was at stake for England was a "cheap and speedy victory in the East, and that better we win and break our word than lose."[29]

Lawrence confirms the British were in a desperate situation in the first half of 1916 when he states that England's "forces were falling back shattered from the Dardanelles" and the "slow-drawn agony of Kut was in the last stage" before the surrender.[30]

In essence, the *Seven Pillars of Wisdom* is a long and lyrical account of how he defrauded and duped the Arabs of the Hijaz to do British bidding during World War One. At one stage in the revolt he wanted to unload the untarnished truth and let Abdullah, the Sharif's son, know that "the promises of Great Britain" to his father were worthless: "I longed to tell him that the half-witted old man had obtained from us no concrete or unqualified undertaking of any sort, and that their ship might founder on the bar of his political stupidity; but that would have been to give away my English masters…"[31]

Lawrence's constant references to the promise of freedom and independence in the book are the ruses he used to persuade the Arabs of the Hijaz to lead this revolt against the Ottoman forces. He knew he had no choice but to be duplicitous because the British Empire had already faced three defeats at the hands of the Ottoman Empire and the Americans had not yet entered the war to rescue the British.

He confirmed his double-dealing as the revolt continued and the fraudulence of his business "stung" him: "I was raising the Arabs on false pretenses, and exercising a false authority over my dupes…"[32]

What's interesting is that Lawrence admits to the struggle of not only deceiving his Arabs but also the struggle of the need to deceive himself: "The war for me held a struggle to side-track thought, to get into the people's attitude of accepting the revolt naturally and trustingly. I had to persuade myself that the British government could really keep the spirit of its promises."[33]

The Arab aspirations were nothing more than a ruse in England's bid to win the war against Germany's ally, the Ottoman Empire. As he cruelly declares: "I exploited their highest ideals and made their love of freedom one more tool to help England win."[34]

Finally, as the revolt drew to a close Lawrence acknowledges that he had been practising a deceit that "others had framed and set a foot" for 2 years.[35]

There is no doubt that if the British Empire had not been defeated at Gallipoli, Kut or its Anglophile protégé Ibn Saud had not been knocked out, the "Arab Revolt" as it is known today, would not have happened. And the revolt was certainly not about adding "much-needed glamour" to World War One as Norman Stone, Professor of International Relations, has stated.[36] Apologists for Lawrence's trickery claim he suffered "prigs of consciousness" because he confesses in his book that he was "duping" Arabs. However, in a world of geo-political manoeuvring admitting one is being duplicitous is not the same thing as admitting one is wrong.

Furthermore, early in the 1920s Lawrence was provided with another opportunity to wear Arab desert garb and showcase his deviousness. Winston Churchill (who had become the Colonial Secretary) sent him on a mission to the Arabian Peninsula. This time it was to bribe and threaten the Sharif of Mecca, the very man who was tricked into doing England's bidding, that if he didn't accept a Zionist-friendly, Anglo-Hijaz treaty with a clause legitimising Britain's colonial project in Palestine, he would inevitably need to contend with a revived Ibn Saud and his Wahhabi henchmen (what today, we would call al-Qaeda).[37]

The Sharif rejected British imperialism's bribes, threats and its colonial Zionist project in Palestine. And on this basis, Ibn

Saud and the Wahhabis were to invade and occupy the Hijaz where they remain to this very day.

Section 2: Britain's Denial of Democracy and the Ethnic Cleansing of Palestine

"The British government have promised that what is called the Zionist movement shall have a fair chance in this country, and the British Government will do what is necessary to secure that fair chance...We cannot tolerate the expropriation of one set of people by another or the violent trampling down of one set of national ideals for the sake of erecting another..."
Winston S. Churchill to an Arab delegation, 30 March 1921.[1]

"I do not admit that the dog in the manger has the final right to the manger, even though he may have lain there for a very long time...I do not admit, for instance, that a great wrong has been done to the Red Indians of America, or the black people of Australia...I do not think the Red Indians had any right to say, "The American Continent belongs to us and we are not going to have any of these European settlers coming in here". They had not the right, nor had they the power."
Winston S. Churchill to the Peel Commission on Palestine, 12th March 1937.[2]

By the end of the official British occupation in Palestine in mid-May 1948, 400,000 Palestinian Arabs had been expelled, directly and indirectly, from the country and 225 villages, towns and centres had more or less been ethnically cleansed of their indigenous inhabitants. Most of the villages were reduced to rubble by the Zionist forces, in order to prevent the indigenous Palestinians from ever returning.

The four hundred thousand that fled during the final 6 months of Britain's rule in Palestine made up half of the indigenous Palestinians that were eventually cleansed by the end of 1948.[3]

The question that inevitably needs to be asked is, what role

Britain played in laying the foundations of what became known as the al-Nakba or the ethnic cleansing of Palestine?

The British Empire obtained eventual control of Palestine and other areas of Arabia by convincing Arabs to side with it, against the Ottoman Empire during World War One. The flags of self-determination and independence were waved by Blighty and proved enough to entice Arabs in Palestine and elsewhere to enter an agreement.

Imperial Britain's agreement with the Arabs is contained in what are known as the Hussain-McMahon letters. So named after the Sharif Hussain bin Ali, leader of the Hijaz region of the Arabian Peninsula and Henry McMahon, the British High Commissioner in Cairo.[4]

Unbeknown to the Arab leadership, Britain made two simultaneous commitments during this period. One was an agreement with the French, known as Sykes-Picot, to carve up the Arab territories under the Ottoman Empire. This agreement is named after the British official Mark Sykes and the French diplomat Francois Georges-Picot. The other was the Balfour Declaration issued from London. This declaration committed the British government to:

"...view with favour the establishment in Palestine of a national home for the Jewish people, and will use their best endeavours to facilitate the achievement of this object..."[5]

At the turn of the twentieth century, 80 per cent of the shipping passing through the Suez Canal belonged to the Empire.[6] Therefore, with Palestine in close proximity to the canal it was thought best to colonise it with European Jews so as to pre-empt any challenge to the British presence in Egypt either from the indigenous Arabs or another foreign power. This was confirmed by C. P. Scott, the legendary *Guardian* editor who reasoned there should be a Zionist state in Palestine because, "Palestine has a special importance for Great Britain because in the hands of a hostile Power, it can be made...a secure base from which a land attack on Egypt can be organised..." As such, it is in Britain's interest that "no Power should be seated in Palestine" that "is likely to be hostile" to British imperialism. Therefore, the British government's deliberate policy is "to encourage in every way in our power Jewish immigration...with a view to the ultimate establishment of a Jewish State."[7] The left-wing *New Statesman* magazine was more forthright on the need for a Zionist colonial-settler state in Palestine. It informed its readers that the "special interest of the British Empire in Palestine is due to the proximity of the Suez Canal." Therefore, in order to establish a "population attached to the British Empire" in Palestine, "a Zionist restoration under British auspices" needs to be fulfilled.[8]

Below, I follow the lead of the historian Professor Walid Khalidi who several years ago in a keynote speech at a conference marking the sixtieth anniversary of the Nakba pointed out that a "hallmark of British policy in Palestine had been the suspension of democracy...Thus the country that is tirelessly hailed in Western capitals today as the sole of democracy in the Middle East came into existence in Palestine only through the burial of democracy."[9] What follows in this chapter are highlights during the period of British rule where democracy was denied to the Palestinians.

What became known as Palestine and is now known as Israel and the occupied Palestinian territories, that is the territory west of the River Jordan, had a population of over 90 per cent Arabs and about 8 per cent Jews upon Britain's entry into the region during World War One. The Arabs formed an overwhelming majority. Clearly representative government in Palestine was a threat to the British-Zionist project and as such needed to be forestalled.

So it is no surprise that David Lloyd George, the then British Prime Minister, in a meeting with Chaim Weizmann, leader of the Zionist movement in the UK, and Lord Balfour, British Foreign Secretary, instructed Winston Churchill, the Colonial

Secretary of the period, that "he mustn't give representative Government to Palestine."[10]

In this same meeting both Balfour and Lloyd George confined and confirmed to Weizmann that by Jewish National Home they actually "meant an eventual Jewish State."[11]

Lord Balfour confirmed that the denial of representative government and democracy was British policy: "In Palestine, we do not propose even to go through the form of consulting the wishes of the present inhabitants of the country..." because Zionism, "be it right or wrong, good or bad, is rooted in age-long tradition, in present needs, in future hopes, of far profounder import than the desires and prejudices of the 700,000 Arabs who now inhabit that ancient land."[12]

The denial of democracy was not only agreed to the governing political party but also supported by the British political opposition, the British Labour Party.

Ramsay MacDonald, the future leader of the Labour Party and the first ever Prime Minister of a Labour government, wrote that Palestinian demands for self-determination were deprived of "complete validity" because the biblical stories he was reared on as a child rendered, "Palestine and the Jew can never be separated."[13] Furthermore, Palestinian Arabs were incapable of developing the resources of their country and as such there is an "alluring call"[14] for "hundreds of thousands of Jews"[15] to colonise Palestine under a British Mandate which sanctimoniously but verily required the denial of representative government to the indigenous Palestinians. Colonel Josiah Wedgwood, a prominent Labour (and former Liberal) politician in the inter-war period, was in favour of democracy in Palestine, but not until the "Jews are in a majority"[16] and once the "higher civilisation" of immigrant Jewish settlers "is numerous and wise enough to make democracy safe for all" they would then be able to "range up beside the other self-governing dominions"[17]of the British empire.

In effect, the founding strategy of Zionism in Palestine was the cross-party British denial of representative government and democracy to the indigenous Arab population.

With this cross-party founding strategy in place, both Conservative and Labour politicians justified Britain's Zionist project, that is to create a Jewish state in Palestine over the heads of the indigenous population, in line with their own ideologies. The Conservatives justified the project with right-wing reasons, while Labour justified with supposedly left-wing reasons.

Firstly, for the British right-wing, Zionist colonialism represented an opportunity to solve a domestic political consideration. Namely, Jewish immigrants or refugees fleeing anti-semitic pograms in eastern Europe. It was concluded, that rather than fleeing to the West, Jews could go to Palestine. As Harry Defries has shown in his book on the Conservative Party's attitude to Jews: "support for a territorial solution for the Jews be it in Palestine or elsewhere, was to find favour with many... who opposed Jewish immigration into Britain."[18]

In an earlier period, Joseph Chamberlain, who claimed that he only despised one race, that is the Jews,[19] found himself agreeing with Theodor Herzl, the founder of Zionism, that the solution is "to find some country in this vast world of ours where these poor exiles can dwell in safety without interfering with the subsistence of others."[20]

Another right-wing justification for the Zionist project was based on pre-empting Jews from joining revolutionary socialist or communist organisations. As Churchill wrote in his essay "Zionism vs Bolshevism," after strongly implying that Jews were responsible for the French and Russian revolutions, he argued it would be "important to foster and develop any strongly-marked Jewish movement which leads directly away from these fatal associations. And it is here that Zionism has such a deep significance..." As such, once "millions" of Jews have migrated to Palestine they "would be especially in harmony with the truest interests of the British Empire," i.e. securing the Suez Canal.[21]

The harmony and security of the British Empire also featured in left-wing justifications for Zionist colonialism. Colonel Wedgwood in his Zionist tract "The Seventh Dominion" wrote that Palestine was geographically the "Clapham Junction" of the British Empire. As such a "friendly and efficient population" is required to settle there. The criteria of the new settlers in Palestine are "men on whom we can depend, if only because they depend on us...The Jews depend on us."[22]

The Wilsonian notion of self-determination was also utilised by the British left-wing to justify the Zionist project. Woodrow Wilson, the American president, had arrived at the peace conference in 1919 brandishing his idealistic strategy to prevent future world conflict and establish peace.[23] The argument had a short shelf life as firstly there were simply not enough Jews in Palestine to determine an independent state and therefore, secondly, even if there were, why should Jewish self-determination be given priority over Arab self-determination?[24] Partly on this basis, Labour politicians reverted to socio-cultural type and imperialist racial dehumanisation. H. N. Brailsford, a former *Guardian* journalist, seconded MacDonald's opinion and justified Zionist colonialism on the basis that the Arabs were incapable of developing Palestine because they were "degenerate semi-savages" who had no right to "exclude millions" of settlers.[25] Representatives of the Labour Party in effect argued that indigenous Arabs were incapable of developing the country and therefore its only hope rested with immigrant Zionist Jews.

From another angle, left-wing justifications were also utilised to misconstrue and belittle Arab opposition to the Balfour Declaration. Following the lead of Zionist labour propagandists, Colonel Wedgwood was at the forefront in arguing that Arab opposition was one based not on self-determination, but on economic class. The Zionists were raising the living standards of the indigenous population and the Arab elite in Palestine were opposed to this development. Wedgwood claimed that the Zionists were "teaching" native Arabs how to claim for higher wages from their elite and this was the source of indigenous opposition to Britain's Zionist project.[26]

In the Anglo-French carve up of the region, the Sykes-Picot agreement, Palestine covers a larger land mass than it does now. The original Palestine entailed the land mass east of the River Jordan, that is now known as the Hashemite Kingdom of Jordan.

The idea to wrench this part of Palestine into a separate entity didn't arise until the very early 1920s. The most popular reason for its creation rotates around the shenanigans of Emir Abdullah, the son of the "duped" Sharif Hussain.[27] The story has it that Abdullah was on his way to what is now known as Syria to liberate it from the French, after they had thrown out his brother Faysal as its ruler.

Therefore to forestall any dispute with its co-imperialist, the British eventually placated Abdullah by making him ruler, firstly on a 6-month probation and then permanently, of this geographical patch of Palestine, the area east of the River Jordan. It became known as Transjordan. However, in the negotiations with the Colonial Secretary Winston Churchill in Jerusalem, Abdullah did ask whether, "His Majesty's Government mean to establish a Jewish kingdom west of the Jordan and to turn out the non-Jewish population?..that men could be cut down and transplanted in the same way as trees."[28]

Churchill denied that this was to be the case. Indeed, he claimed that such assertions were "groundless apprehension among the Arabs in Palestine."[29] Yet Alec Kirkbride, who had served in Transjordan in various capacities[30] since its concoction as well as being an "immense influence"[31] on Emir Abdullah, strongly implies in his autobiography that there may already have been a sinister motive. He states that the country was created because the British had intended it "to serve as a reserve of land for use in the resettlement of Arabs once the National

Home for the Jews in Palestine...became an accomplished fact."[32]

Such an opinion only helps to confirm that the British had intended to ethnically cleanse Palestine of its indigenous population very early into their rule.

By the end of the 1920s, European-Jewish colonial immigration added a further 120,000 settlers to the already 60,000 Jewish inhabitants of Palestine. This was made possible by British imperialism.

In August 1929, major disturbances took hold of Palestine which resulted in the deaths of 133 Jews and 116 Arabs. The British government's then Colonial Secretary, Lord Passfield, launched a commission to investigate the causes of the disturbances. The Shaw Report, so-called after Walter Shaw, reported back to Parliament in March 1930.

The report partly concluded that the disturbances were not pre-meditated and furthermore that the indigenous Palestinians were fearful of their future. Land they had tilled for centuries was being sold by absentee landlords and they were being thrown off by the new Zionist landlords. The new landlords employed only Jewish labour, in accordance with Zionist principles and this had led to apprehension.

Assuredly, certain strategies remained the same. On the eve of the report's publication Lord Passfield confessed to Weizmann that he opposed "a representative legislative council" because he "feared that such elected bodies might become focuses of legal resistance to the proclaimed policy of the Government and the obligations it had undertaken..." i.e. the Balfour Declaration and the commitment to Jewish immigration.[33] And what is Lord Passfield's actual name? Why none other than Sidney Webb, a prominent British Labour socialist, co-founder of the *New Statesman* magazine as well as the co-founder of the London School of Economics.

However, on the back of this report, the government appointed John Hope Simpson to mainly look into how settlement issues in

Palestine could be ameliorated.

While Hope Simpson was conducting his survey in Palestine, Zionist representatives in London met with the Parliamentary Under-Secretary of State for Colonies, Dr Drummond Shiels. Shiels informed the Zionists that Hope Simpson's mission was "to examine the possibilities for settlement of Arab fellaheen (i.e. peasants) in Transjordan and Jews in Western Palestine."[34]

The Shaw Commission's report and the Hope Simpson report remained loyal to British Zionism's gradualist approach in establishing a Jewish majority. This gradualism occasionally came into conflict with the flamboyant Zionism of the representatives of the European settler Jews, who wanted immediate mass immigration into Palestine. Nevertheless, what united British establishment and Jewish Zionists was their agreement to deny representative government to the indigenous Palestinians.[35]

Both of these reports formed the basis of the proposed governmental policy known as the Passfield White Paper of October 1930 which aimed to ostensibly restrict Jewish immigration. Others have had a more cynical interpretation of the reports. The author and son of Mark Sykes, Christopher Sykes, claimed that these reports were a:

"...starting point of a certain rhythm to be noticed from then on in the affairs of Palestine under the Mandate. A Royal Commission goes off to the troubled land; its recommendations lead to the sending of a subsidiary commission to make definitive proposals on how to put the recommendations into effect; the proposals conflict with too much of settled conviction and involve too much political risk to be acted on; both Commissions prove to have been a waste of talent and time. This frequent sending of abortive commissions to Palestine was part of that belief which continues at the present time, namely that if one can only get a clear statement of any problem, its solution must likewise become clear. The belief appears to be true of only a few areas of experience and was never to be true of Palestine."[36]

Indeed, the White Paper was "aborted" in Parliament by Ramsay MacDonald on 13 February 1931 by reading a letter which in effect abrogated the report's findings, therefore continuing the British establishment's commitment to the Balfour Declaration. Implicit in this commitment was the denial of representative government to Palestine.

A Zionist historian has argued that it was this repudiation of the reports in this letter which heralded the mass immigration of the early 1930s. Between 1931 and 1935, Jewish immigration more than doubled to 400,000. [37] Needless to say the horrific and tragic growth of anti-semitism in Europe played no small part in Jews fleeing their homes and seeking salvation in either Palestine or elsewhere.

With the British mandated colonisation of Palestine intensifying, the Palestinians rose up against the Empire and its Zionist-settler proteges in April 1936 in what became known as the 3-year Palestinian Arab Revolt.

Amid the revolt, Britain launched a Royal Commission enquiry. Yet the Colonial Secretary in this period, William Ormsby-Gore, knew all too well what was at the root of the latest disturbances. In June 1936, he stated in Parliament that: "...The Arabs demand a complete stoppage of all Jewish immigration, a complete stoppage of all sales of land, and the transfer of the Government of Palestine...to what they call a National Government responsible to an elected democratic assembly. Those are their three demands, and quite frankly, those demands cannot possibly be conceded."[38]

The Royal Commission was appointed on 29 July 1936; it was headed by Lord Peel and included five other emissaries, including a Professor Reginald Coupland. The results and conclusions of this commission are more commonly known as the Peel Report on Palestine and it reported back to Parliament on 7 July 1937.

The commission had interviewed 66 witnesses and although Arabs did initially boycott the process, by the time they decided to co-operate it may have been too late. On the eve of the Commission meeting its first Arab witness for the report, Coupland informed Weizmann that partition and the establishment of a Jewish state would inevitably be recommended.[39]

It maybe just a case of extreme coincidence that the report's recommendations dovetailed with British intentions, as expressed in private by Lloyd George and Balfour almost 20 years previously, in creating a Jewish state.

Along with partition, the commission also recommended population transfer between Britain's Zionist colonisers and the indigenous population. The report acknowledged that the Palestinians would need to bear the brunt of the population transfer and it also recognised that there are not enough areas for them to be transferred to within Palestine. As the report stated: "It is the far greater number of Arabs who constitute the major problem; and while some of them could be re-settled on the land vacated by the Jews, far more land would be required for the resettlement of all of them."[40]

Note that for the Empire the problem was the indigenous Arabs and not the newly arrived Zionist settlers. Therefore, as Alec Kirkbride informed us in his biography and as Emir Abdullah had originally feared: "...the execution of large-scale plans for irrigation, water-storage, and development in Trans-Jordan...would make provision for a much larger population than exists there at the present time."[41]

The report also deceptively charged that the uprising was due to "present antagonism between the races." That is, the revolt arose from racial conflict and not because Britain continuously denied representative democracy to Palestinians with a view to guaranteeing Zionist immigration and colonisation of Palestine.

The report conclusively envisioned that partition and population transfer, i.e. ethnic cleansing, could be achieved in "less than three years."[42] Just after the publication of the report, Weizmann offered Ormsby-Gore Zionist assistance in transferring the Palestinians of the Galilee to Transjordan.[43]

The report's conclusions heralded not only an intensification of the revolt, but also an intensification of British counter-insurgency operations. As such, it was largely in this period that the "best endeavours" aspect of the Balfour Declaration manifested itself into naked British imperialist military power. The meaning of "best endeavours" now materialised in the military crushing of Palestinian resistance.

Dr Laleh Khalili has written how in this period Palestine became a "hub" for British counter-insurgency methods.[44] That is, these methods were imported from its other colonies such as South Africa or Peshawar in India and then utilised and "consolidated" in Palestine, with the results later to be used in Kenya, Malaya or Oman in the post-World War Two period. Blockhouses, barriers and fences were used to limit or contain population movement. Barbed wire was purchased by Zionist settlers from Mussolini's Italy for the fences.

Doberman dogs from South Africa were imported into Palestine to intimidate Palestinians; the use of human shields which were used in Peshawar, India was incorporated by the British in Palestine. More often than not, when an operation was finished the British vehicle would sharply break, for the Arab to fall off the bonnet and then be deliberately run over.[45]

British officers destroyed, vandalised and looted villages.[46] At times, burning the villages and making a mockery of their hoarded food stuffs.[47] Waterboarding,[48] blowing up a bus full of Arab detainees in a collective punishment reprisal,[49] extrajudicial killings[50] and of course that Balfourian "best endeavour" of them all, robbing children of their pocket money,[51] were all methods utilised by the Empire to crush the revolt. Most importantly though: "the most significant legacy of British counterinsurgency in the Arab Revolt was the training of men who were to become the founding fathers and highest-ranking officers of the Israeli military..."[52]

As such it is difficult not to notice the strong, if not overbearing, similarities between the practices of the Zionist forces in 1947-8 and the British counter-insurgency operations during the Arab revolt of the late 1930s. Some of these practices continue to this day in occupied Palestine.[53]

The revolt was finally crushed in 1939. According to Ghassan Kanafani, the deaths and causalities inflicted on the Palestinians in this period would have been proportionally equivalent to 200,000 Britons killed, 600,000 wounded and 1,224,000 arrested.[54] In other words Palestinian society was politically and militarily decimated.

In the same year, Britain revoked the Peel report as well as another subsidiary report with the 1939 White Paper. Christopher Sykes argued that this was done largely to placate the Arab populations of the Middle East because, "The concern of the Arabic-speaking world with Palestine was not a chimera imagined by orientalists and Arabophils. It was a real fact and an extremely dangerous one."[55] And therefore with an eye on keeping Arabs on side in Imperial Britain's war with Nazi Germany, "...the White Paper...did succeed, very imperfectly but in the main, in its primary object. It cut the ground away from extremist agitators. Slowly rebellion died away in Palestine, and throughout the war years there was no formidable Arab rising against the British in the country."[56]

After the war Britain handed over the Mandate to the United Nations and it is no surprise that although it abstained, it insisted on four commonwealth countries to vote for the partition resolution in November 1947.[57]

The resolution heralded a new chapter in Palestinian history. With the indigenous Palestinians still reeling from the British violence and brutality of the late 1930s, Kanafani argued that the ensuing "civil war" in 1947-8 was merely a belated cleaning up operation by the British-trained Zionist forces. He states the Zionists were plucking "the fruits of the defeat of the 1936 revolt which the outbreak of the war had prevented it from doing sooner."[58]

Can one really be surprised that Britain failed to keep law and order between November 1947 and the official end of the Mandate in May 1948 when half of the actual ethnic cleansing of Palestine took place?

Sixty years later, Lord Balfour's distant successor, the former British Foreign Secretary David Miliband, addressed an Annual Lunch of the Labour Party's Friends of Israel and endorsed the conclusions of the Peel Report. He claimed the then vision to partition Palestine was "good."[59] Naturally, he failed to mention that this "good" vision was and is firmly rooted in Britain's brutal denial of democracy to the indigenous Arab population with a view to establishing a Jewish majority in Palestine. In effect, he endorsed the ethnic cleansing of Palestine so to make way for the creation of the Zionist state in Palestine.

The utilisation of European Jewish suffering in the first half of the twentieth century in arguments to impose Zionist-Jewish immigration and colonialism on Palestine are, if not disingenuous, then certainly incorrect. The British project to colonise Palestine with Zionist Jews predates the intensification of Jewish persecution, the Kristallnacht and the Nazi holocaust.

What mattered to Imperial Britain was the supposed security of the Suez Canal and it wanted to plant what it thought would be a reliable population in Palestine with a view to its security. As the political academic (whose family were early settlers in Palestine) Mayir Verete argued, "the British wanted Palestine – and very much so – for their own interests, and it was not the Zionists who drew them to the country...had there been no Zionists in those days the British would have had to invent them."[60]

It was the supposed security for the Suez Canal that drew the British to Palestine to colonise it. Not Zionists. The Zionists were the tools the British used to accomplish this security. Indeed, from the early 1940s onwards Britain began floating the idea of Zionist-Jewish colonisation of what is now eastern north Africa and specifically Libya, which according to Churchill would then be "linked (if they so chose) with a Jewish home in Palestine."[61] European Zionists did not seem to be as enthusiastic as British imperialists with this idea.[62]

In conclusion, the "only democracy in the Middle East" as Israel's supporters fondly refer to the British engineered colonial entity, is founded not only on ethnic cleansing of the indigenous Palestinian population in 1947-8 but also on Imperial Britain's denial of democracy to the Palestinians during the Mandate period.

Section 3: How Zionism Created the Kingdom of Saudi Arabia

The covert alliance between the Kingdom of Saudi Arabia and the Zionist entity of Israel should be no surprise to any student of British imperialism.

In late 2014, according to the American establishment journal *Foreign Affairs*, the Saudi petroleum minister, Ali al-Naimi, is reported to have said "His Majesty King Abdullah has always been a model for good relations between Saudi Arabia and other states and the Jewish state is no exception."[1] Recently, Abdullah's successor, King Salman, expressed similar concerns to those of Israel to President Obama's agreement between the United States and Iran over the latter's nuclear programme. This led some to report that Israel and KSA presented a "united front" in their opposition to the nuclear deal.[2] This was not the first time the Zionists and the Saudi clan have found themselves in the same corner in dealing with a perceived common foe. In North Yemen in the 1960s, the Saudis were financing a British imperialist led mercenary army campaign against revolutionary republicans who had assumed authority after overthrowing the authoritarian Imam. Gamal Abdul-Nasser's Egypt militarily backed the republicans, while the British induced the Saudis to finance and arm the remaining remnants of the Imam's supporters. Furthermore, the British organised the Israelis to drop arms for the British proxies in North Yemen 14 times.[3] The British, in effect, militarily but covertly, brought the Zionists and Saudis together in 1960s North Yemen against their common foe.

However, as this author has previously written, one must return to the 1920s to fully appreciate the origins of this informal and indirect alliance between Saudi Arabia and the Zionist entity.[4] An illuminating study by Dr Askar H. al-Enazy, titled "The Creation of Saudi Arabia: Ibn Saud and British Imperial

Policy, 1914-1927," has further and uniquely provided any student of British imperialism with primary sourced evidence on the origins of this alliance. This study by Dr Enazy influences the following piece. The defeat of the Ottoman Empire by British imperialism in World War One left three distinct authorities in the Arabian Peninsula: Sharif of Hijaz: Hussain bin Ali of Hijaz (in the west), Ibn Rashid of Ha'il (in the north) and Emir Ibn Saud of Najd (in the east) and his religiously fanatical followers, the Wahhabis.

As mentioned in the first section, Ibn Saud had entered the war early in January 1915 on the side of the British, but was quickly defeated and his British handler, William Shakespear, was killed by the Ottoman Empire's ally Ibn Rashid. This defeat greatly hampered Ibn Saud's utility to the Empire and left him militarily hamstrung for a year.[5] The Sharif contributed the most to the Ottoman Empire's defeat by switching allegiances and leading the so-called "Arab Revolt" in June 1916 which removed the Turkish presence from Arabia. He was convinced to totally alter his position because the British had strongly led him to believe, via correspondence with Henry McMahon, the British High Commissioner in Egypt, that a unified Arab country from Gaza to the Persian Gulf would be established with the defeat of the Turks. The letters exchanged between Sharif Hussain and Henry McMahon are known as the McMahon-Hussain Correspondence.

Understandably, as soon as the war ended, the Sharif wanted to hold the British to their war time promises, or what he perceived to be their war time promises, as expressed in the aforementioned correspondence. The British, on the other hand, wanted the Sharif to accept the Empire's new reality which was a division of the Arab World between them and the French (Sykes-Picot agreement) and the implementation of the Balfour Declaration, which guaranteed "a national home for the Jewish people" in Palestine by colonisation with European Jews. This new reality was contained in the British-written Anglo-Hijaz Treaty, which the Sharif was profoundly averse to signing.[6] After all, the revolt of 1916 against the Turks was dubbed the "Arab Revolt" not the "Hijazi Revolt."

Actually, the Sharif let it be known that he would never sell out Palestine to the Empire's Balfour Declaration; he would never acquiescence to the establishment of Zionism in Palestine or accept the new random borders drawn across Arabia by British and French imperialists. For their part the British began referring to him as an "obstructionist," a "nuisance" and of having a "recalcitrant" attitude.

The British let it be known to the Sharif that they were prepared to take drastic measures to bring about his approval of the new reality regardless of the service that he had rendered them during the war. After the Cairo Conference in March 1921, where the new Colonial Secretary, Winston Churchill, met with all the British operatives in the Middle East, T. E. Lawrence (i.e. of Arabia) was despatched to meet the Sharif to bribe and bully him into accepting Britain's Zionist colonial project in Palestine. Initially, Lawrence and the Empire offered 80,000 rupees.[7] The Sharif rejected it outright. Lawrence then offered him an annual payment of £100,000.[8] The Sharif refused to compromise and sell Palestine to British Zionism.

When financial bribery failed to persuade the Sharif, Lawrence threatened him with an Ibn Saud takeover. Lawrence claimed that "politically and militarily, the survival of Hijaz as a viable independent Hashemite kingdom was wholly dependent on the political will of Britain, who had the means to protect and maintain his rule in the region."[9] In between negotiating with the Sharif, Lawrence made the time to visit other leaders in the Arabian Peninsula and informed them that if they didn't toe the British line and avoid entering into an alliance with the Sharif, the Empire would unleash Ibn Saud and his Wahhabis who after all were at Britain's "beck and call."[10]

Simultaneously, after the conference, Churchill travelled to Jerusalem and met with the Sharif's son, Abdullah, who had been made the ruler, "Emir," of a new territory called "Transjordan." Churchill informed Abdullah that he should persuade "his father to accept the Palestine mandate and sign a treaty to such effect"; if not "the British would unleash Ibn Saud against Hijaz."[11] In the meantime the British were planning to unleash Ibn Saud on the ruler of Ha'il, Ibn Rashid.

Ibn Rashid had rejected all overtures the British Empire made to him via Ibn Saud to be another of its puppets.[12] Moreover, Ibn Rashid expanded his territory north to the new mandated Palestinian border as well as to the borders of Iraq in the summer of 1920. The British became concerned that an alliance might be brewing between Ibn Rashid, who controlled the northern part of the peninsula, and the Sharif, who controlled the western part. More so, the Empire wanted the land routes between the Palestinian ports on the Mediterranean Sea and the Persian Gulf under the rule of a friendly party. At the Cairo Conference, Churchill agreed with an imperial officer, Sir Percy Cox, that "Ibn Saud should be 'given the opportunity to occupy Hail.'"[13] By the end of 1920, the British were showering Ibn Saud with "a monthly 'grant' of £10,000 in gold, on top of his monthly subsidy. He also received abundant arms supplies, totalling more than 10,000 rifles, in addition to the critical siege and four field guns" with British-Indian instructors.[14] Finally, in September 1921, the British unleashed Ibn Saud on Ha'il which officially surrendered in November 1921. It was after this victory the British bestowed a new title on Ibn Saud. He was no longer to be "Emir of Najd and Chief of its Tribes" but "Sultan of Najd and its Dependencies." Ha'il had dissolved into a dependency of the Empire's Sultan of Najd.

If the Empire thought that the Sharif, with Ibn Saud now on his border and armed to the teeth by the British, would finally become more amenable to the division of Arabia and the British-

Zionist colonial project in Palestine, they were disappointed. A new round of talks between the Sharif's son, acting on behalf of his father in Transjordan, and the Empire resulted in a draft treaty accepting Zionism. When it was delivered to the Sharif with an accompanying letter from his son requesting that he "accept reality," he didn't even bother to read the treaty and instead composed a draft treaty himself rejecting the new divisions of Arabia as well as the Balfour Declaration and sent it to London to be ratified![15]

Ever since 1919 the British had gradually decreased Hussain's subsidy to the extent that by the early 1920s they had suspended it, while at the same time continuing to subsidise Ibn Saud right through the early 1920s.[16] After a further three rounds of negotiations in Amman and London, it dawned on the Empire that Hussain would never relinquish Palestine to Great Britain's Zionist project or accept the new divisions in Arab lands.[17] In March 1923, the British informed Ibn Saud that it would cease his subsidy but not without awarding him an advance "grant" of £50,000 upfront, which amounted to a year's subsidy.[18]

In March 1924, a year after the British awarded the "grant" to Ibn Saud, the Empire announced that it had terminated all discussions with Sharif Hussain to reach an agreement.[19] Within weeks the forces of Ibn Saud and his Wahhabi followers began to administer what the British Foreign Secretary Lord Curzon called the "final kick" to Sharif Hussain and attacked Hijazi territory.[20] By September 1924, Ibn Saud had overrun the summer capital of Sharif Hussain, Ta'if. The Empire then wrote to Sharif's sons, who had been awarded kingdoms in Iraq and Transjordan not to provide any assistance to their besieged father or in diplomatic terms they were informed "to give no countenance to interference in the Hedjaz."[21] In Ta'if, Ibn Saud's Wahhabis committed their customary massacres, slaughtering women and children as well as going into mosques and killing traditional Islamic scholars.[22] They captured the holiest place in Islam, Mecca, in mid-October

1924. Sharif Hussain was forced to abdicate and went to exile in the Hijazi port of Akaba. He was replaced as monarch by his son Ali who made Jeddah his governmental base. As Ibn Saud moved to lay siege to the rest of Hijaz, the British found the time to begin incorporating the northern Hijazi port of Akaba into Transjordan. Fearing that Sharif Hussain may use Akaba as a base to rally Arabs against the Empire's Ibn Saud, the Empire let it be known in no uncertain terms that he must leave Akaba or Ibn Saud would attack the port. For his part, Sharif Hussain responded that he had: "never acknowledged the mandates on Arab countries and still protest against the British Government which has made Palestine a national home for the Jews."[23]

Sharif Hussain was forced out of Akaba, a port he had liberated from the Ottoman Empire during the Arab Revolt, on 18 June 1925 on *HMS Cornflower*.

Ibn Saud had begun his siege of Jeddah in January 1925 and the city finally surrendered in December 1925 bringing to an end over 1000 years of rule by the Prophet Muhammad's descendants. The British officially recognised Ibn Saud as the new King of Hijaz in February 1926 with other European powers following suit within weeks. The new unified Wahhabi state was rebranded by the Empire in 1932 as the "Kingdom of Saudi Arabia" (KSA). A certain George Rendel, an officer working at the Middle East desk of the Foreign Office in London, claimed credit for the new name.

On the propaganda level, the British served the Wahhabi takeover of Hijaz on three fronts. Firstly, they portrayed and argued that Ibn Saud's invasion of Hijaz was motivated by religious fanaticism rather than by British imperialism's geo-political considerations.[24] This deception is propounded to this day, most recently in Adam Curtis's acclaimed BBC *Bitter Lake* documentary, where he states that the "fierce intolerant vision of wahhabism" drove the "beduins" to create Saudi Arabia.[25] Secondly, the British portrayed Ibn Saud's wahhabi fanatics as a benign and misunderstood force who only wanted to bring Islam back to its purest form.[26] To this day, these Islamist jihadis are portrayed in the most benign manner regarding their armed insurrections which are supported by Britain and the West such as 1980s Afghanistan or in today's Syria, where they are referred to in the Western media as "moderate rebels."[27] Thirdly, British historians portray Ibn Saud as an independent force and not as a British instrument used to horn away anyone perceived to be surplus to imperial requirements. For example, Professor Eugene Rogan's recent study on the history of Arabs claims that "Ibn Saud had no interest in fighting" the Ottoman Empire. This is far from accurate as Ibn Saud joined the war in 1915. He further disingenuously claims that Ibn Saud was only interested in advancing "his own objectives" which fortuitously always dovetailed with those of the British Empire.[28]

In conclusion, one of the most overlooked aspects of the Balfour Declaration is the British Empire's commitment to "use their best endeavours to facilitate" the creation of "a national home for the Jewish people." Obviously, many nations in the world today were created by the Empire but what makes Saudi Arabia's borders distinctive is that its northern and north-eastern borders are the product of the Empire facilitating the creation of Israel. At the very least the dissolution of the two Arab sheikhdoms of Ha'il and Hijaz by Ibn Saud's Wahhabis is based on their leaders' refusal to facilitate the British Empire's Zionist project in Palestine.

Therefore, it is very clear that the British Empire's drive to impose Zionism in Palestine is embedded in the geographical DNA of contemporary Saudi Arabia. There is further irony in the fact that the two holiest sites in Islam are today governed by the Saudi clan and Wahhabi teachings because the Empire was laying the foundations for Zionism in Palestine in the 1920s. Contemporaneously, it is no surprise that both Israel[29] and Saudi Arabia[30] are keen on militarily intervening on the side of "moderate rebels," i.e. jihadis, in the current war on Syria, a country which covertly and overtly rejects the Zionist colonisation of Palestine.

As the United States, the "successor" to the British Empire in defending Western interests in the Middle East, is perceived to be growing more hesitant in engaging militarily in the region, there is an inevitability that the two nations rooted in the Empire's Balfour Declaration, Israel and Saudi Arabia, will develop a more overt alliance to defend their common interests.

Chapter 6

Origins of the Myth of America's Poodle

"Comrade Johnny lifted his glass to the workers of the world, and then continued with a speech he had just been making to the meeting he had left...American imperialism...the military-industrial machine...Britain's role as lackey...the Vietnam War..."
Doris Lessing, The Sweetest Dream

Beyond any shadow of a doubt, the notion of Great Britain as mere "poodle" to the United States on the global stage emanates from the post-World War Two period. It simply couldn't have happened before World War Two because the British had then bestrode the world as planet earth's leading military and economic imperialist force. As the adage goes, "the sun never set on the British Empire," that is, the sun was always shining on some part of the British Empire. World War Two considerably weakened Great Britain and it is after the war, in the period known as the "Cold War," that the derogative term "poodle" emerged. It is used to denote that the UK is totally subservient to the foreign policy aims of the United States of America. In this chapter I will provide an overview of when this false and misleading derogative specifically took hold.

Origins of the Cold War

In September 1939, four European nations went to war. Adolf Hitler's Germany had invaded Poland and in doing so Britain and France, due to treaty obligations, declared war on Germany. In 1941, Japan attacked the United States military base at Pearl Harbour. Germany, out of solidarity with Japan, declared war on the United States and the latter reciprocated a few days later. This reciprocation made de facto military allies out of, inter alia, the United States and the United Kingdom.

Specifically, Adolf Hitler's plans for European domination based on the ideology of fascism were literally inspired by British imperialism. He aimed to establish a new united European era with a subservient and exploited Russia.

The British Empire's plunder, pillage and impoverishment of India was the template Hitler idealised to model his German Empire or Third Reich. Hitler had declared that British wealth was based on or the "result" of the "exploitation of the three hundred and fifty million Indian slaves." He also argued that what India was to Britain, "the territories of Russia will be for us."[1] The 350 million figure here is presumably what Mr Hitler thought the population of India was at the time of his writing.

At the war's end in 1945, the United States of America emerged as the sole global super power. Also, unlike the rest of the belligerents, the US homeland was untouched by the ravages of war. As for Europe, specifically western Europe, it was the second time in a generation that it had dragged mankind into a global conflict. A glimpse of the horrors that the British, French and Belgian imperialists had visited on less technologically advanced Africans, Asians and South Americans (hereafter the "Global South") over the previous centuries had returned home to roost in the early 1940s.

There is nothing original about this perspective. As poet and politician Aime Cesaire has argued, fascism was not an aberration from European history. It was European history in the Global South brought home. He opined that Hitler administered to Europe what hitherto "had been exclusively for the Arabs of Algeria, the 'coolies' of India, and the 'niggers' of Africa."[2] Furthermore, Professor Noam Chomsky further corroborates this perspective in a discussion about the relationship between a nation-state's domestic and foreign policy: he claims that England "acted like the Nazis" in nineteenth-century India.[3]

It is within this context of European self-destructive meltdown which claimed the lives of tens of millions that the foundations of the Cold War were laid. With western Europe weakened and impoverished, communist political movements gained traction and with the victorious Soviet Union providing a living example of communist rule, the United States was compelled to revive and kick-start the capitalist economies in Europe. Hence, the European Recovery Plan (aka "Marshall Plan") initiative was granted to western Europe to rebuild its economy. As historian Professor Melvyn P. Leffler argued in his essay on the strategy behind the Marshall Plan, the United States "wanted to spawn an economic recovery in western and southern Europe, [to] undermine the appeal of Communist parties..."[4]

The Americans poured billions of dollars into western Europe for them to purchase predominately American goods to reconstruct their economies. Obviously, the Americans were not acting out of pure altruism. The aid provided to western Europe allowed these devasted nations to purchase American goods, and in turn grease the wheels of the American economy. American prosperity was now connected to a revived Europe earning US dollars to purchase American goods. And vice versa, western Europe's prosperity was now also an American economic interest.

In effect, post-war western Europe, the UK included, was, as Chomsky argued in his book *Deterring Democracy*, "reconstituted with much of the traditional order restored, but within the overarching framework of US power."[5] African-American civil rights activists decried their government's position vis-à-vis reviving European capitalism knowing full well it would entail continued European imperialism in Africa and Asia. As civil rights activist Paul Robeson argued:

"...the real meaning of the Marshall Plan is the complete enslavement of the colonies. For how can British, French and other Western European bankers repay Wall Street? Only in raw materials – in gold, copper, cocoa, rubber, uranium, manganese, iron ore, ground nuts, oils, fats, sugar, bananas. From where? Why from South Africa, Nigeria, East Africa, French Africa, Belgian Congo, Trinidad, Jamaica, Cuba, Honduras, Guatemala, Viet Nam, Malaya. The Marshall Plan means enslavement of our people all over the earth…"[6]

For the Marshall Plan to succeed European imperialism in Africa and Asia needed to be maintained. Because war had considerably weakened Europe's hold over its colonies, it was left for the United States to come to the militarily assistance of its European allies. As Chomsky argues,"As for the United States, its intervention in the Third World, particularly in the early years [of the Cold War], was in part impelled by the goal of securing a hinterland for the state capitalist economies that it hoped to reconstruct in Western Europe and Japan."[7]

The Marshall Plan helped to prop up the Western order in the early years after the end of World War Two. Moreover, the ideological confrontation with the Soviet Union needed actual western European economic examples as showcases of the capitalist order guaranteeing prosperity and security far better than communist states under Soviet Union rule could. This could not be done without maintaining the European economic interests in vast areas of the Global South.

It is within this context that we understand why the United States, United Kingdom, France and other western European powers became hostile to Third World nationalist movements who wanted to wrest control of their resources from European imperialism.

Therefore, if we were to unpack the American global hegemony that emerged after World War Two, it can be based on three factors. Firstly, western European white supremacist military self-destruction; secondly, the United States commitment to reconstructing western Europe after the ravages of war – it basically rewarded Europe for dragging mankind into global conflict by guaranteeing its restitution and reconstruction; thirdly, in order for Europe to be an economic success, the United States needed to economically and militarily assist Europe in securing its interests in the Global South. On the final factor, Professor Leffler expresses it as such, "Far from limiting American attention to Europe, the Marshall Plan, along with other considerations, accentuated American interest in those areas around the globe that appeared to be of paramount commercial and financial importance to Britain, France, western Germany" and other recipients of American abundance.[8]

Imperialist Interventions

One of the first tests of this new American order in defence of its allies' interests was when Iran's democratically elected leader, Muhammad Mossadegh, nationalised Iranian oil in the early 1950s. Iran had aroused the ire of Britain's ruling class by openly and transparently discussing the nationalisation of the British oil company Anglo-Iranian Oil Company (AIOC) in its Parliament.

In 1950 AIOC made a £170 million profit, with the British exchequer receiving far more in taxes than the Iranian government in royalties from the company. AIOC was the UK's single largest overseas asset. The original concession to AIOC in 1933 had stipulated that the company did not pay any custom duties or income tax to Iran.[9] Most Iranians found this arrangement highly disagreeable. Moreover, the Iranian leader who put his name to the original agreement lacked legitimacy and was perceived to be nothing but a stooge of the British by his countrymen – and he had admitted as such.[10]

When the government of Iran finally brought Iranian oil under its authority, the socialistic Labour government headed up by Clement Atlee expressed a desire to invade Iran. It drew up a plan, Operation Buccaneer, to capture the oil refineries at Abadan, where the oil was being extracted. When the British put the idea forward to the Democrat President Truman for approval and support, he rejected it. It is said that the Empire was within 3 hours of intervening and capturing Abadan before the mission was aborted.[11]

By nationalising the oil industry, Mossadegh had denied the British state a source of income while it was in the midst of post-war reconstruction which included building the foundations of the new welfare state. Just as importantly, if this nationalisation proved to be successful it might inspire others in the Middle East and beyond to throw off the British imperialist yoke.[12] On this basis, it was only natural that the leader of the Conservative opposition and arch-imperialist Winston Churchill denounced the nationalisation of the oil industry as an "outrage."[13] As author Christopher De Bellaigue writes in his account of the coup: "Patriot of Persia: Muhammad Mossadegh and a Very British Coup," "What Mossadegh and his supporters considered a victory of right over wrong was for the British a theft and a violation."

However, the British persisted and finally got their way with the election of a new Republican president (General Dwight Eisenhower) in January 1953. Correspondingly, Churchill had been back at the helm in the UK for over a year. This time the British played the communist bogeyman card to win over American support. An MI6 officer travelled to the United States to warn of the "dangers of communism"[14] assuming power in Iran. That clinched the deal for the British imperialists.

In return for US support to overthrow Iranian democracy, the British allowed the Americans to "dip their beak" (as the fictional, small time crook Funucci said to the young Vito Corleone in the Godfather novel) in Iranian oil profits. American oil companies were to be guaranteed a 40 per cent stake in Iranian oil on the back of democracy being hanged and overthrown.[15]

After months of planning the United States and the United Kingdom violently overthrew Iranian democracy and with it Mossadegh in a coup d'état called Operation Ajax, on 19 August 1953. This operation reinstalled the Shah dictatorship which lasted until the Iranian revolution of 1979. With Iranian parliamentary democracy out of the way, the British baptised their capitalist fangs in Iran afresh. The name AIOC was cast into the dustbin of history and the phoenix of British Petroleum (now simply BP) arose gloriously draped in the blood of Iranians and murder of Iranian democracy.

"From an American perspective," writes De Bellaigue, "the tragedy of Mossadegh is that the United States allowed itself to become Britain's accomplice and trigger-man."[16] The Americans had assisted the British in maintaining the Empire's interests in Iran in accordance with Cold War doctrine.

Besides the new name given to the British oil company, the ripple effects of this episode are felt to this very day with a tense relationship between the United States and Iran. Furthermore, would the war between Iraq and Iran in the 1980s have happened if the Americans had rejected British wishes to overthrow Iranian democracy? Another fall out from this episode was in West Germany of all places. The Shah's visit to West Germany in 1967 was greeted by student protests. A student was shot dead by the police which led to the further radicalisation of the student protest movement. This radicalisation found ultimate manifestation in the Red Army Faction or the Baader-Meinhoff organisation which led a campaign of anti-capitalist violence for decades.

What's most interesting about the British-initiated coup is that to this very day British politicians and mainstream commentators from all political backgrounds do not acknowledge that it was originally a British plan to overthrow Mossadegh, whereas in the United States even one of their presidents has acknowledged that they overthrew Iranian democracy.[17]

Later in the 1950s, 1956 to be exact, the British concocted a plan with France and its Zionist colonial entity, Israel, to invade and eventually dislodge the popular Egyptian leader Gamal Abd al-Nasser (Nasser). Each state had its own reasons for wanting to rid Egypt of Nasser. The French held him in contempt for his support for the Algerian resistance to their occupation. However, the ultimate pretext for the invasion was when Nasser nationalised the Suez Canal which had sent the British establishment into a frenzy. Nasser had placed the canal under Egyptian control which was unacceptable to the British imperial establishment as it denied their companies and shareholders profits. Nasser also wanted a united Arabia homeland with its (oil) resources prioritised to the needs of the masses rather than British or French interests. Harold Macmillan, a future British Prime Minister, alluded to this during the crisis when he said that without the oil of the Arabian Peninsula, the British nation would be "lost" and the whole structure of the British "economy would collapse." "Without oil," Macmillan noted, "and without the profits from oil," the UK will not be able to survive.[18] Such an assessment is confirmed by Professor David A. Nichols in his biography of President Eisenhower in this period. He argued that, "British anxieties about the Middle East were rooted, in no small part, in the dire financial straits that Anthony Eden's [British Prime Minister] confronted. The British economy had been devasted by World War 2 and, eleven years later, had not fully recovered, in spite of massive American aid."[19]

Furthermore, the Americans knew that "European economies would collapse if Arab oil was cut off."[20]

Moreover, if Nasser, like Mossadegh, were to succeed in this daring act, it might lead to others in the Global South emulating him and nationalising their main industries and revenue streams.

Ultimately, the British and their partners (tripartite) were finally compelled to pull back from the invasion due to both Egyptian resistance and the fact that the tripartite failed to clear their conspiracy with the new leader of the Western world, the United States. The Empire had kept their actual saviour in two world wars blind to their conspiratorial plans.

The Suez invasion taught the British establishment they could no longer initiate large-scale imperialist invasions without first the approval of the United States. This is sometimes referred to as a "humiliation" by historians and media commentators. The end of over two hundred years of British imperialist tradition whereby the British Empire could bomb and invade any country or people in the Global South at will had hit the rocks and was now referred to as "humiliation" or "blunder." However, during this conflict the Americans came to realise that British or generally European prosperity depended on the flow of oil to them so the question was how to prioritise Europe without alienating Arabs. As Eisenhower asked: "What *must* we do in Europe and then the question, how do we square this with the Arabs?"[21]

The American priority in the Middle East was not the people of the region but British and European prosperity.

In early 1958, to counter Nasser's Arab unity ideas, propaganda and the newly formed United Arab Republic of Egypt and Syria, the two British-installed puppet kings, the one in Jordan and the other in Iraq, announced their intention to unite their countries. This intention was literally forestalled with the overthrow of the Iraqi puppet in July 1958 led by regiments in the Iraq Army headed by General Kassim. Feeling threatened, that the overthrow of the British puppet in Iraq would lead to a domino effect which would engulf the British-created order in the Middle East, the Americans, in the name of stability, immediately landed troops in Lebanon, while the British sent troops to Jordan to prop up its puppet leader there. As Macmillan admitted in his biography, if there was a revolutionary coup against their ally in Jordan, then the British "position in the whole area would be threatened" and Jordan may join the United Arab Republic.[22] According to President Eisenhower, the British had further wanted the Americans to lead a more broad invasion of the entire region overthrowing not only the new government in Iraq but also the governments of Syria and Egypt and it was they, the Americans, who needed to rein in any British ideas about a wholescale invasion of the Middle East.[23] Away from the Middle East, Britain was also waging brutal and barbaric wars on the people of Malaya and Kenya in the 1950s.

Fast forward to 1963 in North Yemen, Britain led the way in a counter-revolutionary operation after a group of Nasserite army officers overthrew the feudal ruler, Imam Muhammad al-Badr, and established a republic on 26 September 1962. British mercenaries, green lighted by the government, led the campaign to undermine the new republic. The Americans had complained that "British policy endangered the stability of Saudi Arabia, but Macmillan was not to be deflected."[24]

The North Yemeni tribes, backed by Britain alongside Saudi Arabia, Jordan and Israel, were categorised as "Royalists" as opposed to the "Republicans" backed by Nasser's Egypt. In March 1963, "millions of pounds worth of light weapons, including fifty thousand Lee Enfield rifles, were secretly flown out from an RAF station in Wiltshire" to the Royalists to complement an Israeli arms drop earlier in the month.[25] Simultaneously in South Yemen, British imperialism was involved in counter-revolutionary operations from 1964 onwards and in neighbouring Oman from 1965 where Britain was supporting a slave trading sultanate against revolutionaries who wanted to overthrow the British puppet and his slave-system. Yet British students, when they finally took note about what was being done to preserve the global capitalist system, decided to demonstrate against American imperialism in Vietnam.

1960s Anti-War Demonstrations

The Americans invaded and waged war on Vietnam only after French imperialism failed to crush the Vietnamese people. In order to uphold European interests and prevent the spread of what it perceived to be communism but more precisely self-determination, the United States jumped into the Vietnamese battlefield.

A leading voice of the British demonstrations against the American war in Vietnam was Tariq Ali who had arrived from Pakistan to study in England in the early 1960s but quickly established himself as a leading radical figure. His biography covering this period, *Street Fighting Years: An Autobiography of the Sixties*, is advertised by his publishers as an "autobiography of an entire generation." Tariq's UK political awakening coincided with a new dawn in British politics, that is the election of Harold Wilson's Labour government in 1964. And although, like most politicians, Wilson in opposition made himself electable to anti-imperialists by criticising American foreign policy, once in power he naturally supported the United States' foreign policy in Vietnam. Or as Tariq states: "Wilson became an abject apologist for US foreign policy"[26] and he accuses the Labour leaders of being "tame poodles of the White House."[27]

In 1965, after returning from a visit to Vietnam, Tariq was convinced that "there was one overriding priority for radicals, socialists and democrats in the West. We had to do everything in our power...to help the Vietnamese drive the Americans out of their country."[28] This is unproblematic but why was he so focused on Vietnam rather than British imperialist wars in North Yemen, Aden or Oman. Weren't the progressive elements within these countries fighting for the same ideals as the Vietnamese, that is national self-determination?

Later in the 1960s, at a tribunal in Sweden about the war in Vietnam, one of Tariq's comrades rhetorically asked why the Social Democrat leader of Sweden was totally different to Britain's Labour leader in his opposition to the Vietnam War. Tariq suggests that "the difference might not be one of ideology but strategic location. Britain was a crucial pillar of the NATO alliance..."[29] The problem with this suggestion is that it doesn't take into consideration that the United States bailed out the British elite in two world wars, financed its post-war reconstruction with the Marshall Plan and helped and allowed it to secure its interests in Africa and Asia thereafter. It's nothing to do with location and simply coming to terms with which side of your bread is buttered. It is Tariq's comrade who is ignorant of the history of British imperialism and Tariq for one reason or another, consciously or unconsciously, acquiesces and even indulges him with an answer.

Unlike Latin America and of course Vietnam, Palestine is not an issue for 1960s UK-based radicals. So when the Zionist entity was victorious in the June 1967 war, it was merely a footnote in the history of the decade. The short space Tariq affords the war is handed over to an unabashed Zionist, namely his beloved Trotskyist hero Isaac Deutscher, who Tariq informs the reader had "not been unsympathetic to the foundation of Israel and had known Ben-Gurion well."[30] In other words, Tariq allows for a pro-Zionist ethnic cleanser to speak and provide insights into his conscience about how the Zionist entity should not be over-confident with its victory and that "Israel's security" is not served with this new accomplishment but will only render it more "vulnerable."[31] (To be fair to Tariq, he now speaks more frequently of the Palestinian cause and doesn't seem to have much time for Zionists.)

Many people who have a non-Eurocentric approach to global affairs would argue that Western wealth is based on the enslavement and expropriation of the darker shades of humanity. This book's earlier chapters cover how England's pirates led to the slave trade and opened the doors to the conquest of India. Yet for Tariq, the "wealth of the First World, if properly utilised, could help transform the Third World."[32] This is much more than flawed analysis and a truly shocking statement and in fact no one in the "Third World" wants the wealth of the first world. What mostly should be done is that Western nations stop economically exploiting and waging war (under whatever pretext) on them.

The 1960s anti-war demonstrations reached their zenith in 1968. In London, two major demonstrations took place, one in March and the other later in the year. In both instances there were skirmishes with the police and many arrests as demonstrators battled outside the American embassy. These demonstrations are now part and parcel of the legendry political landscape of anti-war activism. This is all very well, but already mentioned, British imperialism at the time was very much engaged in a series of wars in North Yemen, South Yemen and Oman. There was little, if any, solidarity for the people of the southern Arabian Peninsula as they fought British-backed reactionary forces. Instead of the American embassy shouldn't these demonstrators have been outside the Foreign and Commonwealth Office in Whitehall?

More so, the war that broke out between Irish independence fighters and the British military in the northern part of Ireland in 1969 receives scant attention in Tariq's biography.

One can easily discern from Tariq's book that an entire British era's internationalism or anti-imperialism is defined not by opposition to British foreign policy but American foreign policy. In effect, demonstrations against the US war on Vietnam became the vehicle with which the new anti-imperialist politics expressed itself. This trait can also be seen in Christopher Hitchens' autobiographical account of the period. Once again, his political activist coming of age is partly defined by opposition to the American war on Vietnam. Like Tariq, he had hoped that the Wilson government would distance itself from American foreign policy as he writes, "I had expected the newly elected Labour government to withhold British support for this foul war (and amazingly coarse and thuggish-looking American president who was processing it), and when this expectation was disappointed I began…to experience a furious disillusionment with 'conventional' politics."[33]

Note that the disillusionment is with a British Labour government's support for an American imperialist war of aggression and not any British imperialist aggressions. What's also interesting is that like Tariq, Palestine was not an issue for Hitchens and indeed he adopts a pro-Zionist position vis-à-vis the 6-day war in June 1967. When the war broke out, he had this to say: "...in a war to extinguish the State of Israel. It seemed to me obvious that here was a tiny state, clinging to the seaboard of the Eastern Mediterranean, and faced not with defeat but with existential obliteration. Like many leftists of the time, I sympathised by instinct with the Jewish state."[34]

Joan Bakewell, the BBC broadcaster and journalist, whose strong sympathies with the 1960s anti-war protestors and revolutionaries contributed to her being awarded a peerage and a seat in the unelected chamber of Parliament, the House of Lords, confirmed the centrality of Vietnam to British protestors. She remembers, "Harold Wilson was in power, so everyone complained about him because he didn't denounce the Vietnam War."[35]

The Vietnamese people were fighting for the same ideals as Kenyans, Malayans, Yemenis, Omanis but sadly there were no solidarity demonstrations for the latter group. Also, British imperialist wars on the latter group and the violence administered on them only differed from the American violence in Vietnam in quantity, not quality. As historian Mark Curtis writes in his post-war account of British foreign policy, "Many British policies in the Malayan war were copied with even more devastating effect by the US in Vietnam. 'Resettlement' became the 'strategic hamlet' programme. Chemical agents were used by the British in Malaya for similar purposes as agent orange in Vietnam. Britain had experimented with the use of chemicals as defoliants and crop destroyers from the early 1950s."[36]

One of Tariq's early observations in his biography is of a Labour politician from Atlee's government of left-wing repute travelling to Malaya and "standing triumphantly" as he is photographed, ISIS style, with "decapitated heads of executed communist guerrillas" at his feet.[37] There is no analysis of this episode or why British imperialism was fighting so-called "communist guerrillas" in Malaya. That it may have had something to do with keeping Malayan resources, namely rubber, in British hands seems to be alien to Tariq. Instead, he dismisses the episode as a peculiar episode of a Labour politician moving to the right of the political spectrum rather than as another episode of a British statesman barbarically glorifying in imperialist war on the darker shades of humanity.

The United States war on Vietnam not only killed millions of people but it was the moment the world came to gruesomely recognise that American imperialism had replaced European imperialism as the forefront defender of the capitalist global empire. America's horrific war on Vietnam was seared into the minds of the people of the Global South and many more.

One could argue that when American students and civil rights campaigners railed against their country's war on Vietnam they were holding their country's imperialist establishment to account. But when British students railed and marched against the Vietnam War, they were not holding to account their own country's imperialist establishment. This is not to deny that many British people were horrified by America's war on Vietnam but if British demonstrators were holding their own establishment to account then maybe they should have begun with the already mentioned wars the British establishment waged on indigenous people in many other parts of the world during the 1950s, 1960s and beyond.

Commemorating the fiftieth anniversary of the 1968 European upheavals and uprisings, Tariq had this to say about British imperialism, "the British Labour movement, or at any rate most of it, has always been part and parcel of the empire – it never opposed British imperialism and the colonies. In fact, they were quite superior...thinking of themselves as taking civilisation to them. So there was never a viable anti-imperialist tradition...in British politics."[38]

This beggars the question, if Britain or its "Labour movement" doesn't have an anti-imperialist tradition, then what exactly were the anti-war demonstrations in the 1960s about?

In conclusion, for the 1960s British anti-war generation it was simply a given that the United States, presumably by some act of nature, became the world's leading capitalist and imperialist power. They made no effort to link the American war on Vietnam to the collapse of European white supremacy at the end of World War Two. British and other Western European political and economic elites' dependence on the United States' military power is rooted in their own imperialist decline and brutal self-destruction. It is this history which compels Britain into a close geo-political alliance with the United States and not some mythical notion of beastly subservience to a greater power.

Epilogue

At the end of World War Two, the British establishment emerged economically bankrupt. The British Empire which had up to 1939 prided itself on pillaging and plundering a good proportion of the darker shade of humanity was now dependent on developing a closer relationship with its former colony, the United States of America, in order to guarantee the security of its global interests. It was not only the challenge of Germany, Nazi or otherwise, that made this dependency inevitable but also the manner in which Britain (and other European nations) lost its colonial territories to Japanese imperialism in the Far East. The Japanese had easily militarily overrun the British Empire in Malaya, Singapore, Hong Kong and elsewhere.

The challenge of these two imperialist nations, Germany and Japan, confirmed that Britain was singularly incapable of defending its imperialist interests in far flung reaches of the world. As "socialist" British Prime Minister Clement Atlee argued: "the British Commonwealth and Empire is not a unit that can be defended by itself...The conditions which made it possible to defend a string of possessions scattered over five continents by means of a fleet based on island fortresses have gone."[1] In other words, the nineteenth-century "gunboat" manner in which British imperialism defended its possessions and plunder was over and found wanting by British defeats in the early part of World War Two. British imperialism by itself could no longer hold its own against all types of rising powers.

What was feared at the turn of the twentieth century about empires in lock to a set time period of "rise and fall" materialised in the war. Therefore, the British establishment had no choice but to turn and ingratiate itself with the United States. In effect, the Empire needed to latch itself onto the coat tails of an imperial America. As such, Atlee continued, Britain must now be considered "an easterly extension of a strategic arc the centre of which is the American continent [United States] more than as a power looking eastwards through the Mediterranean and the East."[2]The naval link between the Mediterranean and the East is the Suez Canal and it is mainly for this reason that the British issued the Balfour Declaration in 1917 which paved the way for the British-Zionist ethnic cleansing of Palestine that established the colonial-settler state in close proximity to the canal. As the American civil rights activist and writer James Baldwin once wrote, the "state of Israel was not created for the salvation of the Jews; it was created for the salvation of the Western interests... The Palestinians have been paying for the British colonial policy."[3]

On the other hand, the United States needed a global strategic partner during the Cold War. As Professor Henry Kissinger, the former United States Secretary of State, was to disclose many years later:

"...I thought it was important for America and important for the structure of the world to have another country that independently designed its policy but, because of its own convictions and a maybe different tradition of foreign policy and a longer experience with geopolitics, worked on common conclusions. I thought that that was important for us...That's why I've been in favour of a nuclear capability for Britain because I wanted Britain to be recognised as a significant country in terms of global strategy."[4]

For Great Britain to remain a "significant country," working on "common conclusions" with the United States, that is deterring the spread of communism or what in effect were self-determination movements in the Global South, the British imperialist indirect rule order established in the Middle East in the immediate aftermath of World War One needed to be maintained. And it needed to be maintained to financially guarantee Britain as a "significant country." When this order was challenged by Mossedeq in Iran, Nasser in Egypt and the Arab World as well as in Kenya, Malaya and other parts of the world, Britain was sure of United States support to defend this order. This order, specifically the Arab side of the Persian Gulf, has also reaped immense wealth for the British economy to this day. The descendants of the fratricide desert bandits who are now the puppet rulers of Qatar, Kuwait, UAE, Oman or Saudi Arabia have showered immense wealth on Britain. Whether the puppets are ploughing the oil revenues into British infrastructure projects, sporting entertainment such as football and horse-racing, the financial industry, the military-industrial complex, the education industry or providing a contemporary outlet for surplus British labour in its hundreds of thousands it's no surprise that English, certainly not Arabic, is the lingua franca of this half of the Persian Gulf. The full details and subsidies ("investments") that these puppets provide to the modern British state is beyond the scope of this book.[5] Needless to say that the British pillaged, looted and impoverished India as well as many other parts of the world for many centuries but this did not guarantee permanent economic superiority over other rising nations so therefore the current wealth of the Persian Gulf being poured into the United Kingdom through its puppets will not guarantee continued financial prosperity for British imperialism.

The British establishment's need for a "special relationship" with the United States is an *existential* one in the sense that British imperialism, because of its comprehensive decline, is best defended by the umbrella of a globally driven American military because the British had failed to defend their imperialist interests in World War Two. For the United States a relationship with its former imperial master is based on its own global *strategic* interests. On this basis the very notion that Britain is the United States' "poodle" is totally wrong.

When George Orwell wrote in the 1930s that England's "high standard of life" depended on "a hundred million Indians" living on the verge of starvation under the British Empire and if not the alternative would be "to reduce England to a cold and unimportant little island…and live mainly on herrings and potatoes," he obviously, through no fault of his own, didn't foresee the era when the British establishment became of strategic importance to the new imperial American global hegemony.[6]

British (and European) economic prosperity during the early years of the Cold War depended on keeping much of the Global South in a subservient position to London and other western European capitals. Hence, this is why someone like the Congolese leader Patrice Lumumba was overthrown by the United States, Belgium and Britain.

The 1960s anti-war generation defined anti-imperialism, whether consciously or unconsciously, as opposition to solely American imperialism. This generation was disappointed with the then Prime Minister Harold Wilson's position on the United States' war on Vietnam. As such, at this moment of history, this generation dubbed Wilson's Britain a "poodle" of the United States. But this "poodle" jibe doesn't take into account that Britain was historically central or laid the foundations to the genocides, enslavements, dispossession, impoverishment and ethnic cleansing of whole swathes of nations among them Black Africans, indigenous Americans, indigenous and enslaved Caribbeans, Irish, Indians, the aboriginals of Australia, Palestinians and the list could go on. Within this historical context, the "poodle" jibe is a cruel and false absurdity. In effect, consciously or unconsciously, the notion that Wilson, a Blair or a Cameron is a "poodle" of American power allows for the de-historisation of contemporary British militarism by individualising the reason behind a military intervention. So rather than locating a current imperialist adventure within the history of British imperialism, it is disingenuously located within the (servile) agency of whoever happens to be the British Prime Minister.

Moreover, false pretexts to wage war are nothing new to British imperialism and indeed are older than Britishness itself. One could argue that it began with the false "letters of reprisals" as a justification for England's pirates to loot Portuguese and Spanish shipping during the first Elizabethan reign, then there was the lie of the "Black Hole of Calcutta" to justify war on Bengal, followed by accusing the ruler of Awadh (in India) of tyranny only for its people to rise up against British imperialism after Awadh was annexed in the 1850s. In the modern era, the crushing of the great Palestinian revolt against the British Empire and their Zionist-settler proteges in the mid-1930s was partly justified on the basis that the Palestinians were taking instructions from Mussolini, the Italian fascist leader. Most recently in the second Elizabethan reign, the British establishment was at the forefront in informing the world that Saddam Hussain's Iraq had weapons of mass destruction, that Britain was "45 minutes" away from being attacked and that Saddam was purchasing uranium from Niger. In the run-up to the war on Libya, British media led the way with lurid false accusations against the government of Colonel Gaddafi in that he was committing atrocities and employing African mercenaries high on viagra to kill his own people. Then Foreign Secretary William Hague also falsely insinuated that Gaddafi had fled to Venezuela.

The "War on Terror" launched in 2001 by George W. Bush's United States has allowed (like the preceding "Cold War" and "New World Order") Britain to continue its imperialist tradition to wage war or at the very least delegitimise, destabilise and undermine countries that had escaped British imperialist hegemony. This explains why Britain was just as eager as the United States in military intervention in Iraq in 2003 and more eager when it came to regime change in Libya in 2011 and supporting extreme Islamists in the war on the Syrian nation-state.

Endnotes

Chapter 1

1. Mark Curtis, Secret Affairs: Britain's Collusion with Radical Islam (London: Serpent's Tail, 2018), pg. 228.
2. http://www.cryptome.org/qadahfi-plot.htm (accessed 7 February 2018).
3. Martin Chulov, "SAS and MI6 officers released by Libya's rebel commanders" The Guardian, 7 March 2001. https://www.theguardian.com/world/2011/mar/07/sas-mi6-released-libya-rebels, accessed on 8 March 2018.
4. Jon Swaine and Bruno Waterfield, "UN Plans sanctions to turn up heat for Gadhaffi", Daily Telegraph, 26 February 2011.
5. Deborah Hayne, "Britain ready to use force to free Libya", The Times, 1 March 2011.
6. Robert Winnett, James Kirkup, Nick Meo and Bruno Waterfield "The West is ready to Use Force against Gadhaffi", Daily Telegraph, 1 March 2011.
7. James Kirkup and Richard Spencer, "Army ready for Libyan mission...", Daily Telegraph, 5 March 2011.
8. Christopher Hope, "Cameron plan for no-fly zone shunned by world leaders", Daily Telegraph, 2 March 2011.
9. Editorial, "Waiting for Washington", The Times, 26 February, 2011.
10. Editorial, "Essence of Indecision", The Times, 4 March, 2011.
11. David Charter, Roland Watson and Giles Whittel, "Britain pushes US to agree no-fly zone", The Times, 10 March 2011.
12. Anne Applebaum, "Libya: Gaddafi is about to force Barack Obama's hand", Daily Telegraph, 11 March 2011.
13. Matthew D'Ancona, "David Cameron knows what to do about Libya, but does Obama?", Sunday Telegraph,

13 March 2011.

14. Editorial, "America's silence is hurting the West", Daily Telegraph, 17 March, 2011.

15. Editorial, "Leadership Needed", The Times, 16 March 2011.

16. Phillippe Naughton and Deborah Haynes, "Cameron calls for 'leadership' on Libya as rebels lose ground", The Times, 16 March 2011 and Editorial, "America's silence is hurting the West", Daily Telegraph, 17 March, 2011.

17. Editorial, "Deserted by Obama", The Times, 17 March 2011.

18. House of Commons Foreign Affairs Committee, "Libya: Examination of intervention and collapse and the UK's future policy options", House of Commons, 14 September 2016.

19. Patrick Wintour, "Boris Johnson refuses to apologise for Libyan 'dead bodies' remark" The Guardian, 17, October, 2017. https://www.theguardian.com/politics/2017/oct/17/ boris-johnson-refuses-to-apologise-for-libyan-dead-bodies-remark (accessed, 8 March 2018).

20. Niall Ferguson, "The British Prime Minister is Coming to America", Newsweek, 12 March 2012, http://www. newsweek.com/british-prime-minister-coming-america-63655 (accessed 2nd July 2018).

21. Peter Foster and Jon Swaine, "David Cameron congratulates 'my friend Barack Obama' as he wins Second Term in White House", Daily Telegraph, 7 November 2012, http://www. telegraph.co.uk/news/worldnews/us-election/9660476/ David-Cameron-congratulates-my-friend-Barack-Obama-as-he-wins-second-term-in-White-House.html (accessed 2nd July 2012).

22. Justyna Pawlak and Peter Griffiths, "EU to consider all options to help Syrian rebels", Daily Star, 14 December 2012, http://www.dailystar.com.lb/News/Middle-East/2012/Dec-14/198502-cameron-syria-is-facing-a-desperate-situation-inaction-is-not-an-option.ashx#axzz2K257UuTN (accessed

2nd July 2018).

23. Bob Woodward, "Plan of Attack", (London: Simon and Schuster, 2004), pg 428-429.

24. Tim Sculthorpe, Ben Glaze and Theo Usherwood, "Syrian arms embargo to be reviewed", The Independent, 17 December 2012, http://www.independent.co.uk/news/world/middle-east/syrian-arms-embargo-to-be-reviewed-8422796.html (accessed 2nd July 2018).

25. Steven Erlanger, "Syrian Opposition Leader confers with US and Russia" New York Times, 2 February 2013, http://www.nytimes.com/2013/02/03/world/middleeast/syrian-opposition-leader-confers-with-us-and-russia.html?_r=0 (accessed 2nd July 2018).

26. Vickram Dodd, Nicholas Watt and Richard Norton Taylor, "45 minute claim on Iraq war hearsay", The Guardian, 16 August 2003, https://www.theguardian.com/politics/2003/aug/16/davidkelly.iraq (accessed 2 July 2018).

27. BBC News, "White House warned over Iraq claim", BBC News Channel, 9 July 2003, http://news.bbc.co.uk/1/hi/world/americas/3056626.stm (accessed 2nd July 2018).

28. Andrew Murray and Lindsey German, "Stop the War", (London: Bookmarks Publications, 2005), "Foreword by Tony Benn."

29. ibid., pg.198.

30. Quoted in Miles Erwin, "Whitehall protest ban imposed for Bush Visit", The Metro, 11 June 2008, https://metro.co.uk/2008/06/10/whitehall-protest-ban-imposed-for-bush-visit-182277/ (accessed 2nd July 2018).

31. Seamus Milne "Throwing your Weight About" The Guardian, 11 September 2000, https://www.theguardian.com/world/2000/sep/11/sierraleone.comment (accessed on 9 February 2018).

32. Rob D. Kaiser and Michael McGuire, "Blair Unveils Bold Intervention Doctrine", The Chicago Tribune, 23

April 1999, http://articles.chicagotribune.com/1999-04-23/news/9904230097_1_blair-third-world-debt-cold-war (accessed on 9 February 2018).

33. Seamus Milne "Can the US be defeated", The Guardian, 14 February 2002, https://www.theguardian.com/world/2002/feb/14/usa.comment (accessed on 9 February 2018).

34. Seamus Milne, "We are sleeping into a reckless war of aggression", The Guardian, 27 September, 2002, https://www.theguardian.com/world/2002/sep/27/iraq.comment (accessed on 9 February 2018).

35. Seamus Milne, "A war that can't be won", The Guardian, 21 November 2002, https://www.theguardian.com/world/2002/nov/21/terrorism.comment (accessed on 9 February 2018).

36. Seamus Milne, "Direct action may become a necessity", The Guardian, 16 January 2003, https://www.theguardian.com/world/2003/jan/16/iraq.foreignpolicy (accessed on 9 February 2018).

37. Seamus Milne, "The recolonization of Iraq cannot be sold as liberation", The Guardian, 30 January 2003, https://www.theguardian.com/politics/2003/jan/30/foreignpolicy.iraq (accessed on 9 February 2018).

38. Seamus Milne, "The opponents of war on Iraq are not the appeasers", The Guardian, 13 February 2003, https://www.theguardian.com/world/2003/feb/13/iraq.nato (accessed on 9 February 2018).

39. Paul Waugh, Mary Dejevsky and Rupert Cornwell, "Rumsfeld: US may have to launch war without Britain", 12 March 2003, http://www.independent.co.uk/news/world/politics/rumsfeld-us-may-have-to-launch-war-without-britain-122420.html (accessed on 9 February 2018).

40. Bob Woodward, "Plan of Attack", (Simon & Schuster, London, 2004), pg. 338.

41. Seamus Milne, "Blair is plunging Britain into a crisis of

democracy", The Guardian, 13 March 2003, https://www. theguardian.com/world/2003/mar/13/iraq.politics (accessed on 9 February 2018).

42. Seamus Milne, "Iraqis have paid the blood price for a fraudulent war", The Guardian, 10 April 2003, https:// www.theguardian.com/politics/2003/apr/10/foreignpolicy. iraq (accessed on 9 February 2018).

43. Seamus Milne, "A system to enforce imperial power will only be resisted", The Guardian, 28 February 2008, https:// www.theguardian.com/commentisfree/2008/feb/28/ kosovo.iraq (accessed on 9 February 2018).

44. David Smith, "Tony Blair plotted military intervention in Zimbabwe, claims Thabo Mbeki", The Guardian, 27 November, https://www.theguardian.com/world/2013/nov/27/tony-blair-military-intervention-zimbabwe-claim (accessed on 9 February 2018).

45. "British plan to oust Saddam drawn up two years before invasion", The Independent, 1 February 2010, (accessed 13th August 2018).

46. Angela Monaghan, "BP hires former MI6 boss Sir John Sawers", The Guardian, 14 May 2015, https://www. theguardian.com/business/2015/may/14/bp-hires-former-mi6-boss-john-sawers-oil (accessed 2nd July 2018).

Chapter 2

1. Matt Ridley, "Britain must make sure that India is a friend", The Times, 20 March 2017.

2. Gideon Rachman, "Brexit reinforces Britain's imperial amnesia", Financial Times, 27 March, 2016.

3. Niall Ferguson, "Empire: How Britain Made the Modern World" (London: Penguin Books, 2004), pg. 379-380.

4. Susan Ronald, "The Pirate Queen: Queen Elizabeth I, Her Pirate Adventures and the Dawn of Empire", (New York: Harper Perennial, 2007), pg. 41.

5. David Childs, "Tudor Sea Power: The Foundation of Greatness" (Barnsley: Seaforth Publishing, 2009), pg. 15.

6. Kenneth Andrews, "Trade, Plunder and Settlement: Maritime enterprise and the genesis of the British Empire, 1480-1630", (Cambridge: Cambridge University Press, 1984), pg. 11.

7. Ronald, op. cit., pg. 61.

8. Nick Hazlewood, "The Queen's Slave Trader", (New York: William Morrow, 2004), pg. 15.

9. Noam Chomsky, "Pirates and Emperors" (London: Pluto Press, 2016), pg. xiii.

10. Childs, op. cit., pg. 181.

11. Andrews, op. cit., pg. 28.

12. Ronald, op. cit., pg. 61-62.

13. ibid., pg. 82.

14. Peter Earle, "The Pirate Wars" (London: Methuen Publishing Ltd, 2004), pg. 18.

15. Ronald, op. cit., ibid, pg. 62.

16. Ferguson, op. cit., pg. 3.

17. Hazlewood, op. cit., pg. 173.

18. ibid., pg.65-68 and Ronald op. cit., pg. 71.

19. Hazlewood, op. cit., 104-105.

20. Hazlewood, op. cit., 75.

21. ibid, pg.91.

22. Ronald op. cit., g.81.

23. ibid., pg. 89-90 and Hazlewood pg. 101-103.

24. Hazlewood, op. cit., 123.

25. Andrews op. cit., pg.126; Ronald op. cit., pg. 120 and Hazlewood op. cit., pg. 221-222.

26. Ronald op. cit., pg. 61-62.

27. ibid, pg. 116.

28. ibid., pg. 99.

29. John Sugden, "Sir Francis Drake", (London: Barrie & Jenkins, 1990), pg. 19.

30. Ronald op. cit., pg. 107-108.
31. Sugden op. cit., pg. 45 and Ronald pg. 145 and chapter 15 in its entirety distinguishes between Hawkins and Drake.
32. Sugden op. cit., pg. 52.
33. Ronald op., cit., pg. 170.
34. Ronald op. cit., pg 173.
35. ibid., pg. 173 and Andrews op. cit., 63-65.
36. Ronald op. cit., pg. 175.
37. ibid., pg. 178.
38. ibid., pg. 20 and pg. 201.
39. ibid., pg. 201.
40. ibid., pg. 215.
41. ibid., pg. 220-221.
42. ibid., pg. 224.
43. ibid., pg. 224.
44. Andrews op. cit., pg. 154.
45. Ronald op. cit., pg. 227 and Andrews op. cit., pg 154.
46. Ronald op. cit., pg 227-230.
47. ibid., pg. 231.
48. Philip Hatfield, "The Search for the Northwest Passage", History Today, February 2017, pg.11-17.
49. Andrews op. cit., pg. 155.
50. ibid., pg. 156.
51. Ronald op. cit., pg. 232.
52. ibid., pg. 233-236 and Andrews op. cit., pg. 157-158.
53. Andrews op. cit., pg. 166.
54. Kenneth Andrews "Drakes Voyages" (New York: Charles Scribner's Sons, 1967), pg. 82.
55. ibid., pg. 84.
56. ibid., pg. 85.
57. Roland, op., cit., pg. 249.
58. D. B. Quinn, "Ralegh and the British Empire", (Middlesex: Penguin Books, 1973), pg. 63. Kenneth Andrews, "Elizabethan Privateering: English Privateering During the

Spanish War, 1585-1603" (London: Cambridge University Press), pg. 188-191.

59. Quinn, op., cit., pg. 139-140.

60. Roland, op., cit., pg. 291.

61. Andrews, Elizabethan Privateering, op., cit., pg.4 and Ferguson, op., cit., pg. 11.

62. Roland, op., cit., pg. 342.

63. Andrews, Trade, Plunder and Settlement, op., cit., pg. 251-252.

64. Ronald, op. cit., pg. xix.

65. Eric Williams, "Capitalism and Slavery", (Chapel Hill & London: The University of Carolina Press, 1994), pg. 39.

66. David Olusoga, "The history of British slave ownership has been buried: now its scale can be revealed", The Observer, Sunday 12 July 2015, https://www.theguardian.com/world/2015/jul/12/british-history-slavery-buried-scale-revealed, (accessed 4 July 2018).

67. Williams, op. cit., Chapter 5 and Peter Fryer, "Black People in the British Empire: An Introduction" (London: Pluto Press, 1989), pg. 5-12.

68. J. A. McIlroy, "Thatcher drums Drake's message", The Daily Telegraph, 28 October 1989.

69. Andrew Murray and Chris Nineham, "The War on Terror Ten Years on", (London: Stop the War Coalition, 2011), pg.6.

Chapter 3

1. Malcolm X, "The Autobiography of Malcolm X" (London: Penguin Books, 2007), pg. 272.

2. Nick Robins, "The Corporation That Changed the World: How the East India Company Shaped the Modern Multinational" (London: Pluto Press, 2012), pg. 103.

3. ibid., pg. 43, 45.

4. ibid.

5. ibid., pg. 51 and Partha Chatterjee, "The Black Hole of

Empire: History of Global Practice of Power" (Princeton: Princeton University Press, 2012), pg. 36-37.

6. Robins, op. cit., pg. 71-72.

7. Chatterjee, op. cit., pg. 15.

8. ibid., pg. 16 and Michael Fisher, "Indirect Rule in India: Residents and the Residency System 1764-1858" (Oxford: Oxford University Press, 1991), pg. 145.

9. Chatterjee, op. cit., pg. 26.

10. Robins, op. cit., pg. 68.

11. Chatterjee, op. cit., pg. 30-31 and Mudhusree Mukerjee, "Churchill's Secret War: The British Empire and the Ravaging of India during World War 2" (New York: Basic Books, 2010), pg. xii.

12. ibid., pg. 160-167 for how the myth of the "Black Hole" developed in British imperial history.

13. Robins, "The Corporation That Changed the World", pg. 7.

14. ibid., pg. 66.

15. ibid., pg. 66.

16. ibid., pg. 75 and pg. 77-78.

17. Robins, op. cit., pg. 68.

18. ibid., pg. 81 .

19. ibid., pg. 80, pg. 4 and Mukerjee, op. cit., xiii.

20. ibid., pg. 3 (2010 exchange rate).

21. ibid., pg. 77.

22. ibid., pg. 77 and Chatterjee, op. cit., pg. 41. Mukerjee, op. cit., pg. xiii.

23. Ferguson, op. cit., pg. 37.

24. Robbins, op. cit., pg. 152 and 108.

25. ibid., pg. 93.

26. Mukerjee, op. cit., pg. xv-xvi.

27. Robins, op. cit., pg. 94 and Chatterjee, op. cit., pg. 56.

28. Fisher op. cit., pg. 30 and see pg. 164.

29. Fisher op. cit., pg. 6.

30. ibid., pg. 10.

31. ibid., pg. 61-62.

32. ibid., pg. 132.

33. ibid., pg. 136.

34. ibid., pg. 164 and 194-197.

35. ibid., pg. 195-196 and Chatterjee, op. cit., pg. 200.

36. Robins, op. cit., pg.,194, 213, 283.

37. Mukerjee, op. cit., xxii.

38. Chatterjee, op, cit., pg. 197.

39. ibid., pg. 198.

40. Quoted in ibid., pg. 208 and see also Fisher, op. cit., pg. 262.

41. ibid., pg. 210.

42. ibid., pg. 211.

43. Thomas R. Metcalf, "The Aftermath of Revolt: India 1857-1870" (New Delhi: Manohar Publications, 1990), pg. 61.

44. Metcalf, op. cit., pg. 70 and pg. 87.

45. ibid., pg. 299 and Shashi Tharoor, "Inglorious Empire: What the British Did to India" (London: Hurst & Company, 2017), pg. 101.

46. Ferguson, op. cit., pg. 51.

47. Kathryn Tidrick, "Empire & the English Character" (London: I B Tauris & Co, 1992), pg. 25.

48. ibid.

49. ibid., pg. 26.

50. Christopher Herbert, "War of No Pity: The Indian Mutiny and Victorian Trauma" (Princeton: Princeton University Press, 2008), pg. 2, 58, 60, 100.

51. Ferguson, op. cit., pg. 150.

52. ibid., pg. 151.

53. ibid., pg. 33 and see pg. 203.

54. ibid., pg. 87,155, 49.

55. ibid., pg. 156-7, 201.

56. ibid., pg. 176.

57. Randeep Ramesh, "India's secret history: 'A holocaust, one where millions disappeared...'", The Guardian, 24 August

2007, www.theguardian.com/world/2007/aug/24/india.
rand eepramesh, (accessed 6 June 2018).

58. Metcalf op. cit., pg. 219.

59. ibid., pg. 222.

60. Fisher, op. cit., pg. 264.

61. ibid., pg. 224 and pg. 448-449.

62. ibid., pg. 440 and pg. 455.

63. Fisher, op. cit., pg. 10.

64. Robins op. cit., pg. 183.

65. Mukerjee, op. cit., pg. 48.

66. Tharoor, op. cit., pg. 8.

67. Mike Davis, "Late Victorian Holocausts: El nino Famines and the Making of the Third World" (London: Verso, 2010), pg. 13.

68. Tharoor, op. cit., pg. 150.

69. ibid., pg. 152.

70. ibid., pg. 151-162.

71. ibid., pg. 111-123.

72. Fisher, op. cit., pg. 44.

73. ibid., pg. 1, pg. 23, pg. 33, pg. 440, and pg. 460-471 and Ferguson, op. cit., pg. 230.

74. Rosemarie Said Zahlan, "The Creation of Qatar" (London: Croom Helm, 1979), pg. 29.

75. Ravinder Kumar, "India and the Persian Gulf Region, 1857-1907: A Study in British Imperial Policy" (London: Asia Publishing House, 1965), pg. 18 and James Onley, "Britain's Informal Empire in the Gulf, 1820-1971" Journal of Social Affairs, Vol. 22, No. 87, Fall 2005, pg. 31-32.

76. Quoted in ibid., pg. 49.

77. ibid., pg. 106.

78. Quoted in ibid, pg. 125.

79. Patrick Wintour, "Bahrain paying for Royal Navy base despite human rights criticism", The Guardian, 15.6.2016 at https://www.theguardian.com/world/2016/jun/15/bahrain-

paying-royal-navy-base-human-rights-criticism (accessed on 6.1.2018).

80. Fisher, op. cit., pg. 194-195.

81. Fawaz bin Muhammad al-Khalifa, "Today's opening of the Royal Navy's new Bahrain base seriously enhances Britain's ability to defend the Gulf", The Daily Telegraph, 10.11.2016 accessed at http://www.telegraph.co.uk/news/2016/11/10/todays-opening-of-the-royal-navys-new-bahrain-base-seriously-enh/ (on 6.1.2018).

82. Zahlan, op. cit., pg. 33.

83. ibid., pg. 42.

84. ibid., pg. 43-44.

85. ibid., pg. 48.

86. ibid.

87. James Robertson, "Qatar: Buying Britain by the Pound", BBC News website, 9 June 2017, https://www.bbc.co.uk/news/business-40192970 (accessed 12 June 2018) and Rhiannon Curry, "Qataris own more of London than the Queen", The Telegraph, 17 March 2017, https://www.telegraph.co.uk/business/2017/03/17/qataris-london-queen/ (accessed 12 June 2017).

88. Zahlan, op. cit., pg. 128.

89. Gary Troeller, "The Birth of Saudi Arabia: Britain and the Rise of the House of Saud" (London: Frank Cass, 1976), pg. 8 and Kumar op. cit., 138.

90. Troeller, op. cit., pg. 9.

91. ibid., pg. 20.

92. Zahlan, op. cit., pg. 54.

93. Kumar, op. cit., pg. 75-76.

94. ibid., pg., pg. 82-84.

95. Quoted in Zahlan op. cit., pg. 234.

96. Abdel Razzaq Takriti, "Monsoon Revolution: Republicans, Sultans, and Empires in Oman, 1965-1976" (Oxford: Oxford University Press, 2016), pg. 23.

97. Mark Curtis, "Secret Affairs: Britain's Collusion with Radical Islam" (London: Serpent's Tail, 2018), pg. 65-99 and Robert Dreyfus, "Devil's Game; How the United States helped unleash Fundamentalist Islam" (New York: Metropolitan Books, 2005), pg. 65-93.

98. Takriti, op. cit., pg. 19.

99. ibid.

100. David Holden, "The Persian Gulf: After the British", Foreign Affairs 1971, Vol. 49 (4), pg. 735.

101. ibid., pg. 724.

102. Stephen M. Walt, "The Curious case of small Gulf states", Foreign Policy, 12 November 2012, www. http://foreignpolicy.com/2012/11/12/the-curious-case-of-small-gulf-states/ (accessed 6 June 2018).

103. Holden op. cit., pg. 728.

104. ibid.

105. Frank Gardener, "'East of Suez': Are UK forces returning?", 29 April 2013, BBC News (accessed at, http://www.bbc.co.uk/news/uk-22333555 on 11 August 2017).

106. Curtis, op. cit., chapter 21.

Chapter 4

1. Tony Blair, "Tony Blair's Speech to the US Congress", The Guardian, 18 July 2003, https://www.theguardian.com/politics/2003/jul/18/iraq.speeches (accessed 18 June 2018).

2. Robert Cecil, "The Confederate Struggle and Recognition", Quarterly Review, 112 (1862), pg. 554 . I would like to thank Professor Duncan Bell for this reference in an email correspondence in January 2014.

3. ibid., pg. 535-570.

4. Mary Ellison, "Support for Secession: Lancashire and the American Civil War", (Chicago: University of Chicago Press, 1972), pg. 116 and pg. 126-127.

5. ibid., pg. 30-31 and pg. 152 and Thomas E Sebrell "Lincoln's

British Enemies" BBC History Magazine, March 2011, pg. 22-29.

6. Ellison op. cit., pg. 105.
7. Sebrell op. cit., pg. 26-27.
8. ibid., pg. 27.
9. ibid., pg. 28.
10. Ellison op. cit., pg. 59.
11. ibid., pg. 84 and pg. 183.
12. Sebrell, op. cit., pg. 29.
13. ibid., pg. 29.
14. Ellison op. cit., pg. 188.
15. J. A. S. Grenville, "Lord Salisbury and Foreign Policy: the Close of the Nineteenth Century", (London: The Athlone Press, 1970), pg. 55.
16. Howard Temperley, "Britain and America Since Independence", (Basingstoke: Palgrave, 2002), pg. 77-78.
17. Daniel Hannan, "How We Invented Freedom and Why It Matters", (London: Head of Zeus, 2013), pg. 352.
18. Grenville, op. cit., pg. 207.
19. ibid., pg. 209.
20. ibid pg. 202.
21. Niall Ferguson, "Empire: How Britain Made the Modern World", (London: Penguin Books, 2004), pg. 278-281.
22. Aaron Friedberg, "The Weary Titan: Britain and the Experience of Relative Decline, 1895-1905", (New Jersey: Princeton University Press, 1988), pg. 26.
23. Clive Ponting, "Churchill", (London: Sinclair-Stevenson, 1994), pg. 215.
24. Grenville, op. cit., pg. 25.
25. Duncan Bell, "The Idea of Greater Britain: Empire and the Future of World Order, 1860-1900", (Princeton: Princeton University Press, 2007), pg. 36-37.
26. ibid., pg. 225.
27. ibid., pg. 207, pg. 213 pg. 221-222.

28. Ferguson, op. cit., pg. 247-248.
29. Bell, op. cit., pg. 232.
30. ibid., pg. 229.
31. ibid., pg. 209.
32. ibid., pg. 257.
33. Christopher Hitchens, "Blood, Class and Nostalgia", (London: Vintage, 1991), pg. 221.
34. Peter Clarke, "The English-Speaking Peoples before Churchill", Britain and the World, Edinburgh University Press, September 2011, pg. 225.
35. Grenville, op. cit., pg. 373.
36. ibid., pg. 379.
37. ibid.
38. ibid., pg. 422.
39. ibid., pg. 403.
40. ibid., pg. 403.
41. Walter Millis, "Road to War America, 1914-1917"; Quoted in H.C. Peterson, "Propaganda For War: The Campaign Against American Neutrality, 1914-1917", (Port Washington, New York: University of Oklahoma Press, 1968), pg. 6.
42. Peterson, op. cit., pg. 14.
43. ibid., pg. 35.
44. ibid., pg. 266.
45. Ponting op. cit., pg. 216.
46. Martin Gilbert, "The Churchill Papers, Volume: At the Admiralty September 1939-May 1940" (London: Heinemann, 1993), speech to lobby journalists 29.2.1940, pg. 832.
47. Ferguson, op. cit., pg. 348.
48. Ponting op. cit., pg. 320.
49. Hitchens, op, cit., pg. 21.
50. Richard Toye, "Churchill's Empire: The World that Made Him and the World He Made", (London: Pan Books, 2011), pg. 136.

Chapter 5. Section 1

1. T. E. Lawrence "Seven Pillars of Wisdom: A Triumph", (Harmondsworth: Penguin Books, 1983), pg. 566.
2. Adam Hochschild, "Colonial Folly, European Suicide", New York Times, 28 July 2014, https://www.nytimes.com/2014/07/29/opinion/adam-hochschild-why-world-war-i-was-such-a-blood-bath.html?_r=0 (accessed 8 June 2018).
3. Kristian Coates Ulrichsen, "The First World War in the Middle East", (London: Hurst & Company, 2014), pg. 79.
4. ibid.
5. David French, "The Dardanelles, Mecca and Kut: Prestige as a Factor in British Eastern Strategy, 1914-1916", War & Society, 5 (1), May 1987, pg. 49.
6. Ulrichsen, op., pg. 80.
7. French, op. cit., pg. 51.
8. ibid.
9. Ulrichsen, op., pg. 82.
10. The (London) Times, "Doomed Youth", 25 April 2015, https://www.thetimes.co.uk/article/doomed-youth-cvznjhs9brn (accessed 8 June 2018).
11. ibid., pg. 84.
12. ibid., pg. 89.
13. ibid.
14. H. V. F. Winstone, "Captain Shakespear, A Portrait" (London: Quartet Books, 1978), pg. 196-197.
15. Quoted in ibid., pg. 205.
16. ibid., pg. 216.
17. ibid.
18. Lawrence, op. cit.,pg. 266.
19. Gary Troeller, "The Birth of Saudi Arabia", (London: Frank Cass, 1976), pg. 91.
20. Eugene Rogan, "The Arabs: A History", (London: Penguin

Books, 2009), pg. 220.

21. Troeller op. cit., pg. 81.

22. Ulrichsen, op., cit., pg. 132.

23. ibid., pg. 133.

24. Lawrence, op. cit., pg. 59.

25. ibid pg. 26.

26. ibid., pg. 61.

27. Christopher Hitchens, "Hitch-22: A Memoir" (London, Atlantic Books, 2011), pg. 111.

28. Martin Gilbert, "The Churchill Papers, Volume: At the Admiralty September 1939-May 1940" (London: Heinemann, 1993), speech to lobby journalists 29.2.1940, pg. 832.

29. Lawrence op. cit., pg. 24.

30. ibid., pg. 51.

31. ibid., pg. 220.

32. ibid., pg. 387.

33. ibid., pg. 458.

34. ibid., pg. 560.

35. ibid., pg. 569.

36. Norman Stone, "Spoils of Victory", Literary Review, May 2016, https://literaryreview.co.uk/spoils-of-victory (accessed 8 June 2018).

37. Askar H. al-Enazy, "The Creation of Saudi Arabia: Ibn Saud and British Imperial Policy, 1914-1927" (London: Routledge, 2010), pg. 109 and 111.

Chapter 5. Section 2

1. PRO FO 371/6343.

2. Quoted in Angela Clifford, "Serfdom or Ethnic Cleansing? – A British Discussion on Palestine – Churchill's Evidence to the Peel Commission (1937), (Belfast and London: Athol Books, 2003), pg. 34.

3. For an account of the ethnic cleansing that took place under

the British Mandate see Rosemarie M. Esber, "Under the Cover of War", (Alexandria (V.A): Aribicus Books and Media, 2009). For an account of the entire ethnic cleansing see Ilan Pappe, The Ethnic Cleansing of Palestine, (Oxford: Oneworld Publications, 2007).

4. George Antonious, The Arab Awakening, (Florida: Simon Publications, 2001), Appendix A and D.

5. Christopher Sykes, "Cross Roads to Israel", (London: Collins, 1965), pg. 15.

6. Roger Adelson, "London and the invention of the Middle East, 1902-1920"(London: Yale University Press, 1995), pg. 32.

7. The Guardian, 9 November 1917.

8. New Statesman, 17 November 1917.

9. Professor Walid Khalidi, "From 1947 to 1897: From Partition to Basle", Palestine Conference: The Nakba: Sixty Years of Dispossession, Sixty Years of Resistance, London School of Oriental and African Studies (SOAS), 21 February, 2009. https://youtu.be/PxY1oUmpsqw?t=326 (accessed 13 June 2018).

10. Randolph Churchill, "Winston S. Churchill – Companion Volume 4, Part 3", (London: Heinemann, 1977), pg. 1559.

11. ibid. Meeting took place in July 1921.

12. Quoted in Sykes, op. cit. pg. 17 and Khalidi quotes this in his lecture at SOAS.

13. Ramsay MacDonald, "A Socialist in Palestine", Jewish Socialist Labour Confederation – Poale Zion, 1922, pg. 18.

14. ibid., pg. 17.

15. ibid., pg. 19.

16. Josiah Wedgwood, "The Seventh Dominion", (London: The Labour Publishing Company Limited, 1928), pg. 4.

17. ibid., pg. 33.

18. Harry Defries, "Conservative Party Attitudes to Jews", (London: Frank Cass, 2001), pg. 32.

19. ibid., pg. 24.
20. ibid, pg. 45.
21. Winston Churchill, "Zionism vs. Bolshevism", Illustrated Sunday Herald, (London), 8 February 1920. http://www.fpp.co.uk/bookchapters/WSC/WSCwrote1920.html (accessed 14 June 2011).
22. Wedgwood. op. cit. pg. 3.
23. Margaret Macmillan, The Peacemakers, (London: John Murray, 2003), pg. 19-21.
24. Paul Kelemen, "Zionism and the British Labour Party: 1917-1939", Social History, Vol. 21, No.1, January 1996, pg. 73.
25. ibid.
26. Commons Debates, Fifth Series, Vol. 143, Column 307, 14 June 1921.
27. T. E. Lawrence ("of Arabia") quoted in Ma'an Abu Nowar, "The History of the Hashemite Kingdom of Jordan: Vol. 1", (Oxford: Icatha Press, 1989), pg. 10.
28. CAB 24/126.
29. ibid.
30. Abu Nowar, op. cit., pg. 25, pg. 31, pg. 172 and pg. 195.
31. Ilan Pappe, Britain and the Middle East Conflict 1948-1951, (London: Macmillan Press, 1988), pg. xii
32. A. S. Kirkbride, "A Crackle of Thorns", (London: John Murray, 1956), pg. 19.
33. Joseph Gorny, "The British Labour Movement and Zionism", (London: Frank Cass and Company Limited, 1983), pg. 69.
34. ibid., pg. 72.
35. ibid., pg. 72-75.
36. Sykes, op. cit. pg. 144.
37. Gorny, op. cit. pg. 103-104.
38. Commons Debates, Fifth Series, Vol. 313, Column 1324, 19 June 1936.
39. Sykes, op. cit. pg. 192 and pg. 198-203.
40. Report of the Palestine Royal Commission, Cmd. 5479

(London, 1937), pg. 391.

41. ibid.

42. ibid.,pg. 39

43. 43. Philip Mattar, "The Mufti of Jerusalem: Al-Hajj Amin al-Husayni and the Palestinian National Movement", (New York Columbia University Press, 1988), pg. 81.

44. Laleh Khalili, "The Location of Palestine in Global Counterinsurgencies", International Journal of Middle East Studies, Vol. 42, Issue 3(2010), pg. 413-433.

45. Matthew Hughes, "The Banality of Brutality: British Armed Forces and the Repression of the Arab Revolt in Palestine, 1936-1939", English Historical Review, 124 (2009), pg. 329.

46. ibid., pg. 320-322.

47. ibid., pg. 338-339.

48. ibid., pg. 331.

49. ibid., pg. 337.

50. ibid., pg. 347.

51. ibid., pg. 328.

52. Khalili, op. cit., pg. 418.

53. ibid. For example Khalili draws attention to the destruction of the old city of Jaffa by the British in the 1930s and recent Israeli practices in the "West Bank" of Palestine, specifically, Jenin.

54. Ghassan Kanafani, 'The 1936-39 Revolt in Palestine', (London: Tricontinental Society, 1980), pg. 27. http://www.newjerseysolidarity.org/resources/kanafani/kanafani4.html (accessed 14 June 2011).

55. Sykes, op. cit., pg. 238.

56. ibid pg. 239.

57. Professor Walid Khalidi, "From 1947 to 1897: From Partition to Basle", Palestine Conference: The Nakba: Sixty Years of Dispossession, Sixty Years of Resistance, London School of Oriental and African Studies, 21st February, 2009. The author was present. Indeed, the first time I heard, in a blunt

manner, that Israel was based on the denial of Palestinian democracy was here.

58. Kanafani, op. cit., pg. 30.
59. David Miliband, "Prospects in the Middle East", Annual Lunch of Labour Friends of Israel, London, 4 November 2008. http://davidmiliband.net/speech/prospects-in-the-middle-east/ (accessed 13th June 2011).
60. Mayir Verete, "From Palmerston to Balfour: Collected Essays of Mayir Verete", (London, Frank Cass, 1992), pg. 3-4.
61. Gorny, op. cit. pg. 175. British Labour Party support for "throwing open Libya...to Jewish settlement" (Hugh Dalton, British Chancellor 1945-47) see John Callaghan, "The Labour Party and Foreign Policy: A History" (London: Routledge, 2007), pg. 158.
62. For a British discussion of this initiative see, W. R. Louis, Imperialism at Bay, (Oxford: Oxford University Press, 1977), pg. 58-62.

Chapter 5. Section 3

1. Asher Orkaby, "Rivals With Benefits: Israel and Saudi Arabia's Secret History of Cooperation", Foreign Affairs, 13th March 2015, https://www.foreignaffairs.com/articles/middle-east/2015-03-13/rivals-benefits (accessed 14 June 2018).
2. Richard Spencer, "Israel and Saudi Arabia present united front over Iran deal", The Daily Telegraph, 14 July 2015, https://www.telegraph.co.uk/news/worldnews/middleeast/iran/11739349/Israel-and-Saudi-Arabia-present-united-front-over-Iran-deal.html (accessed 14 June 2018)
3. Orkaby, op. cit.
4. Nu'man Abd al-Wahid, "British Origins of Modern Violent Islamism", Black Commentator, 11 September 2008,

http://blackcommentator.com/290/290_islamo_fascism_
britishism_al_wahid_guest.html (accessed 14 June 2018).

5. Gary Troeller, "The Birth of Saudi Arabia" (London: Frank
    Cass, 1976) pg. 91.

6. Askar H. al-Enazy, "The Creation of Saudi Arabia: Ibn Saud
    and British Imperial Policy, 1914-1927" (London: Routledge,
    2010), pg. 105-106.

7. ibid., pg. 109.

8. ibid., pg. 111.

9. ibid.

10. ibid.

11. ibid., pg. 107.

12. ibid., pg. 45-46 and pg. 101-102.

13. ibid., pg. 104.

14. ibid.

15. ibid., pg. 113.

16. ibid., pg. 110 and Troeller, op. cit., pg. 166.

17. al-Enazy op. cit., pg. 112-125.

18. al-Enazy, op. cit., pg. 120.

19. ibid., pg. 129.

20. ibid., pg. 106 and Troeller op. cit., 152.

21. al-Enazy, op. cit., pg. 136 and Troeller op. cit., pg. 219.

22. David Howarth, "The Desert King: The Life of Ibn Saud"
    (London: Quartet Books, 1980), pg. 133 and Randall Baker,
    "King Husain and the Kingdom of Hejaz" (Cambridge: The
    Oleander Press, 1979), pg. 201-202.

23. Quoted in al-Enazy op. cit., pg. 144.

24. ibid., pg. 138 and Troeller op. cit., pg. 216.

25. Adam Curtis, "Bitter Lake", BBC, https://www.youtube.
    com/watch?v=VRbq63r7rys (accessed 14 June 2018). This
    segment begins towards the end at 2 hrs 12 minutes 24
    seconds.

26. al-Enazy op. cit., pg. 153.

27. Patrick Cockburn, "Obama's Moderate Rebels Are Nowhere

to Be Found", The Real News, 12 September 2014, https://
therealnews.com/stories/pcockburn0912isis (accessed 14
June 2018).

28. Eugene Rogan, "The Arabs: A History", (London: Penguin
    Books, 2009), pg. 220.

29. Christa Case Bryant, "UN reports Israeli support for Syria
    rebels", Christian Science Monitor, 7 December 2014, https://
    www.csmonitor.com/World/Middle-East/2014/1207/UN-
    reports-Israeli-support-for-Syria-rebels (accessed 14 June
    2018).

30. Laila Bassam and Tom Perry, "Saudi Arabia's 'intensified'
    support to Syrian rebels is reportedly slowing regime
    advances", Business Insider, 6 November 2015, http://
    uk.businessinsider.com/saudi-arabias-intensified-support-
    to-syrian-rebels-is-reportedly-slowing-regime-advances-
    2015-11?r=US&IR=T (accessed 14 June 2018).

Chapter 6

1. Quoted in Niall Ferguson, "Empire, How Britain Made the
   Modern World", (London: Penguin Books, 2004), pg. 334.

2. Aime Cesaire, "Discourse on Colonialism" (New York:
   Monthly Review Press, 2000), pg. 36.

3. Noam Chomsky, "Chomsky explains Cold War in 5 min",
   YouTube, 25 November 2010, https://www.youtube.com/
   watch?v=j9Z05xyGB0c&feature=youtu.be&t=38 (accessed 3
   July 2018).

4. Melvyn P. Leffler "The United States and the Strategic
   Dimensions of the Marshall Plan", Diplomatic History,
   Volume 12, Issue 3, 1988, pg. 277.

5. Noam Chomsky, "Deterring Democracy" (London: Vintage,
   1992) pg. 46.

6. Speech by Paul Robeson, "For Freedom and Peace", New
   York, 19 June 1949 transcribed in "Paul Robeson Speaks:
   Writings, Speeches, Interviews 1918-1974" (London:

Quartet Books, 1978), pg. 207.

7. Chomsky op. cit., pg. 23.

8. Leffler, op. cit., pg. 278.

9. Christopher De Bellaigue, "Patriot of Persia: Muhammad Mossadegh and a Very British Coup", (London: Vintage Books, 2013), pg. 97 and pg. 117.

10. ibid., pg. 73.

11. ibid., pg. 169 and James Cable, Intervention at Abadan: Plan Buccaneer, (London: Macmillan, 1991),pg. ix.

12. ibid., pg. 183.

13. De Bellaigue, op. cit., pg. 165.

14. ibid., pg. 221.

15. Stephen Dorril, "MI6", (London: Forth Estate, 2000), pg. 583 and John Keay, "Sowing the Wind", (London: John Murray,

16. 2003) pg. 415..

17. De Bellaigue, op. cit., pg. 5-6.

18. Jason Ditz, "Obama Admits to US Role in Iran Coup", Antiwar.com, 4 June 2009, https://news.antiwar.com/2009/06/04/obama-admits-to-us-role-in-iran-coup/ (accessed 7 June 2018).

19. Alistair Horne, "Macmillan 1894-1956 Volume 1 of the Official Biography" (London: Macmillan, 1988) pg. 411,422 and 429 respectively.

20. David A. Nichols, "Eisenhower 1956, The President's Year of Crises" (New York: Simon & Schuster, 2011), pg. 70.

21. ibid., pg. 88.

22. ibid., pg. 270.

23. Harold Macmillan, "Riding the Storm 1956-1959" (London: Macmillan, 1971), pg. 517.

24. William B. Quandt, "Lebanon 1958, Jordan 1970" in Barry M. Blechman and Stephen S. Kaplan (eds) "Force without War" (Washington DC: The Brookings Institution,1978) pg. 239.

25. Stephen Dorril, "MI6: Fifty Years of Special Operations"

(London: Forth Estate, 2000), pg. 684.

26. ibid.

27. Tariq Ali, "Street Fighting Years: An Autobiography of the Sixties", (London, Collins, 1987) pg. 45.

28. ibid., pg. 46.

29. ibid., pg. 61.

30. ibid., pg. 124.

31. ibid., pg. 158.

32. ibid., pg. 158-9.

33. ibid., pg. 180.

34. Christopher Hitchens, "Hitch-22: A Memoir" (London, Atlantic Books, 2011), pg. 81.

35. ibid., pg. 358.

36. Joan Bakewell, "The World Was Never the Same", Spiked-Online, May 2018, http://www.spiked-online.com/spiked-review/article/the-world-was-never-the-same#.W0EqdNJKjIU (accessed 7 July 2018)

37. Mark Curtis, "Web of Deceit: Britain's Real Role in the World" (London: Vintage Books, 2003), pg. 342.

38. Ali, op. cit., pg. 32.

39. Tariq Ali (with David Edgar), "That was the year that was", London Review of Books, 24 May 2018, pg. 3-10.

Epilogue

1. Niall Ferguson, "Empire: How Britain Made the Modern World" (London, Penguin Books, 2004), pg. 358.

2. ibid.

3. James Baldwin, "Open Letter to the Born Again", The Nation, 29 September 1979. Reprinted on 23 July 2014. (https://www.thenation.com/article/open-letter-born-again/), accessed 15 August 2018.

4. Henry Kissinger, "The Henry Kissinger interview: the Transcript" Prospect Magazine, 18 September 2014, http://www.prospectmagazine.co.uk/other/henry-kissinger-

interview-the-transcript, accessed 04.06.2018

5. Jamie Robertson, "Qatar: Buying Britain by the Pound", BBC News, 9 June 2017, https://www.bbc.co.uk/news/business-40192970 (accessed 28 August 2018) and Nu'man Abd al-Wahid, "London's Shard and the Arab World's Sectarianism", Churchill's Karma, 4 April 2015, https://churchills-karma.com/2015/04/04/arab-worlds-sectarianism-and-the-london-shard-2/ (accessed 28 August 2018).

6. George Orwell, "The Road to Wigan Pier", (London: Penguin Books, 1989), pg. 148.

CULTURE, SOCIETY & POLITICS

Contemporary culture has eliminated the concept and public figure of the intellectual. A cretinous anti-intellectualism presides, cheer-led by hacks in the pay of multinational corporations who reassure their bored readers that there is no need to rouse themselves from their stupor. Zer0 Books knows that another kind of discourse – intellectual without being academic, popular without being populist – is not only possible: it is already flourishing. Zer0 is convinced that in the unthinking, blandly consensual culture in which we live, critical and engaged theoretical reflection is more important than ever before.
If you have enjoyed this book, why not tell other readers by posting a review on your preferred book site.
Recent bestsellers from Zero Books are:

In the Dust of This Planet
Horror of Philosophy vol. 1
Eugene Thacker
In the first of a series of three books on the Horror of Philosophy,
In the Dust of This Planet offers the genre of horror as a way of thinking about the unthinkable.
Paperback: 978-1-84694-676-9 ebook: 978-1-78099-010-1

Capitalist Realism
Is there No Alternative?
Mark Fisher
An analysis of the ways in which capitalism has presented itself as the only realistic political-economic system.
Paperback: 978-1-84694-317-1 ebook: 978-1-78099-734-6

Rebel Rebel
Chris O'Leary
David Bowie: every single song. Everything you want to know, everything you didn't know.
Paperback: 978-1-78099-244-0 ebook: 978-1-78099-713-1

Cartographies of the Absolute
Alberto Toscano, Jeff Kinkle
An aesthetics of the economy for the twenty-first century.
Paperback: 978-1-78099-275-4 ebook: 978-1-78279-973-3

Malign Velocities
Accelerationism and Capitalism
Benjamin Noys
Long listed for the Bread and Roses Prize 2015, *Malign Velocities* argues against the need for speed, tracking acceleration as the symptom of the ongoing crises of capitalism.
Paperback: 978-1-78279-300-7 ebook: 978-1-78279-299-4

Meat Market
Female Flesh under Capitalism
Laurie Penny
A feminist dissection of women's bodies as the fleshy fulcrum of capitalist cannibalism, whereby women are both consumers and consumed.
Paperback: 978-1-84694-521-2 ebook: 978-1-84694-782-7

Poor but Sexy
Culture Clashes in Europe East and West
Agata Pyzik
How the East stayed East and the West stayed West.
Paperback: 978-1-78099-394-2 ebook: 978-1-78099-395-9

Romeo and Juliet in Palestine
Teaching Under Occupation
Tom Sperlinger
Life in the West Bank, the nature of pedagogy and the role of a
university under occupation.
Paperback: 978-1-78279-637-4 ebook: 978-1-78279-636-7

Sweetening the Pill
or How We Got Hooked on Hormonal Birth Control
Holly Grigg-Spall
Has contraception liberated or oppressed women? *Sweetening
the Pill* breaks the silence on the dark side of hormonal
contraception.
Paperback: 978-1-78099-607-3 ebook: 978-1-78099-608-0

Why Are We The Good Guys?
Reclaiming your Mind from the Delusions of Propaganda
David Cromwell
A provocative challenge to the standard ideology that Western
power is a benevolent force in the world.
Paperback: 978-1-78099-365-2 ebook: 978-1-78099-366-9

Readers of ebooks can buy or view any of these bestsellers by
clicking on the live link in the title. Most titles are published
in paperback and as an ebook. Paperbacks are available in
traditional bookshops. Both print and ebook formats are available
online.
Find more titles and sign up to our readers' newsletter
at http://www.johnhuntpublishing.com/culture-and-politics
Follow us on Facebook
at https://www.facebook.com/ZeroBooks
and Twitter at https://twitter.com/Zer0Books